QUIET MOMENTS
ALONE WITH GOD

PRESENTED TO

PRESENTED BY

DATE

QUIET
MOMENTS
ALONE
with GOD

QUIET
MOMENTS
ALONE
with GOD

BETHANYHOUSE

MINNEAPOLIS, MINNESOTA

Quiet Moments Alone With God
Copyright © 2006 by GRQ, Inc.

Published by Bethany House Publishers
11400 Hampshire Avenue South
Bloomington, Minnesota 55438

Bethany House Publishers is a division of Baker Publishing Group, Grand Rapids, Michigan.

Scripture quotations noted CEV are taken from THE CONTEMPORARY ENGLISH VERSION. Copyright © 1991 by the American Bible Society. Used by permission.

Scripture quotations noted ESV are from The Holy Bible, English Standard Version, copyright © 2001 by Crossway Bibles, a division of Good News Publishers. Used by permission. All rights reserved.

Scripture quotations noted GOD'S WORD are from *God's Word,* a copyrighted work of God's Word to the Nations Bible Society. Copyright © 1995 by God's Word to the Nations Bible Society. Used by permission. All rights reserved.

Scripture quotations noted MSG are taken from *THE MESSAGE: The New Testament, Psalms and Proverbs.* Copyright © 1993, 1994, 1995 by Eugene H. Peterson. All rights reserved.

Scripture quotations noted NASB are taken from the NEW AMERICAN STANDARD BIBLE® Copyright © 1960, 1962, 1963–1968, 1971, 1973–1975, 1977, 1995 by the Lockman Foundation. Used by permission.

Scripture quotations noted NCV are from The Holy Bible, New Century Version, copyright © 1987, 1988, 1991 by Word Publishing, a division of Thomas Nelson, Inc. All rights reserved. Used by permission.

Scripture quotations noted NIV are taken from the *Holy Bible: New International Version* (North American Edition)®. Copyright © 1973–1978, 1984, by the International Bible Society. Used by permission of Zondervan. All rights reserved.

Scripture quotations noted NKJV are taken from THE NEW KING JAMES VERSION. Copyright © 1979, 1980, 1982, Thomas Nelson, Inc., Publishers.

Scripture quotations noted NLT are taken from the *Holy Bible,* New Living Translation, copyright © 1996. Used by permission of Tyndale House Publishers, Inc., Wheaton, Illinois 60189. All rights reserved.

ISBN 978-0-7642-0289-6
Compiler and Editor: Lila Empson
Associate Editor: Natasha Sperling
Writers: Patrick and Donna Schlachter
Design: Whisner Design Group

*God's Spirit touches our spirits and confirms
who we really are. We know who he is, and
we know who we are: Father and children.*

Romans 8:16 MSG

CONTENTS

INTRODUCTION

Living and seeking God's presence in your life is an attitude of the heart. In some ways, it's like scuba diving. Because you can get all turned around under water, you can't rely on how you feel. You learn to stop, breathe, think, and then act.

 In your spiritual walk with God, you must also rely on things you can't see, including God's promises to you through the Bible. As you travel this road of faith, you must first seek him, then breathe the Bible into your life and meditate on it. Finally, you put what you learned into action.

This book welcomes you into a journey of discovery, where you will learn how to live in God's presence while you seek his plan for your life. Plan to spend some time getting to know the God who wants you to stop, breathe, think, and act out his very best for you.

SEEKING GOD'S LOVE

Don't let anyone think less of you because you are young. Be an example to all believers in what you teach, in the way you live, in your love, your faith, and your purity.

1 Timothy 4:12 NLT

DRESSED AND READY TO GO

*Be ready! Let the truth be like a belt around your waist,
and let God's justice protect you like armor.*
EPHESIANS 6:14 CEV

It's important to wear the right clothes for the right activity. You wouldn't go hiking in your best

shoes or go ice skating on skis. The right clothes make the activity comfortable, safe, and enjoyable.

When you walk the path that God has set before you, wearing the right spiritual clothing will make you more comfortable, will make the journey of faith safer, and will let you enjoy your walk with God. Choose to be clothed in God's truth and righteousness, and you will walk strong and straight. Even those everyday hindrances will seem as nothing when God is with you.

*God, when the path seems crooked and I stumble, remind
me that you are always just ahead of me leading the way.*
AMEN.

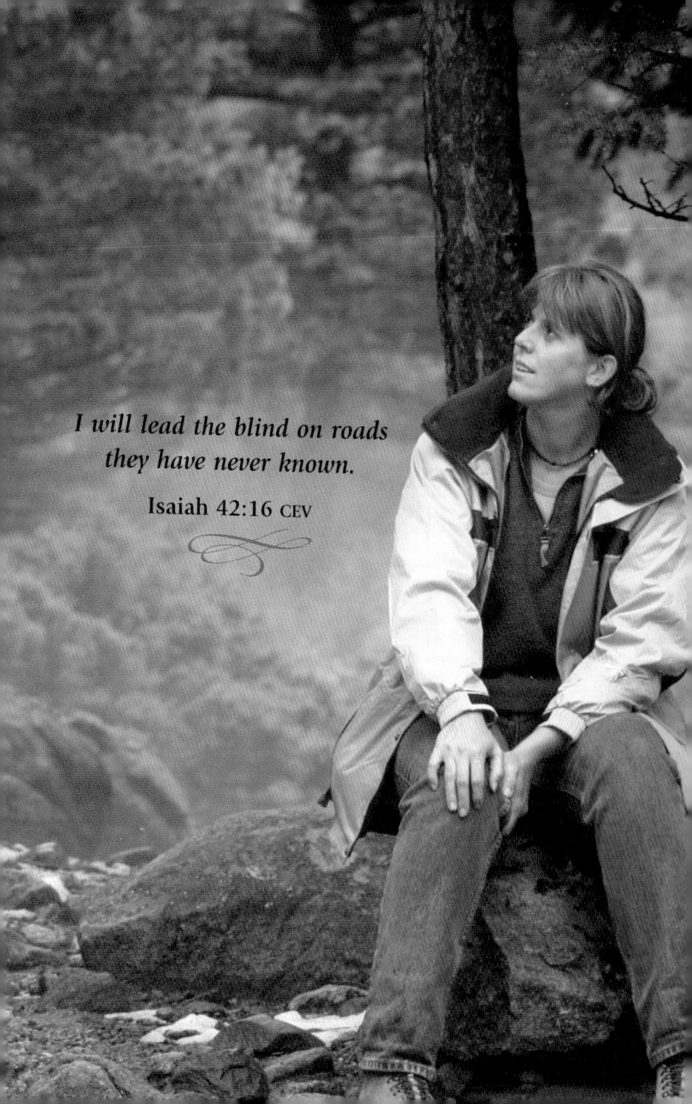

I will lead the blind on roads
they have never known.

Isaiah 42:16 CEV

UNENDING PATIENCE

You, O God, are both tender and kind, not easily
angered, immense in love, and you never, never quit.
PSALM 86:15 MSG

Winston Churchill was asked to deliver the graduation speech at his former high school. The audience

settled in for a lengthy talk. Sir
Winston stared into the faces of
the students. His baritone voice
echoing throughout the auditori-
um, he said, "Never, never, never
quit." With that, he sat down, con-
cluding the shortest graduation
speech in history.

God created Sir Winston and you in his image.
God's love for you surpasses anything you can ever do.
He loves you more than you can imagine. Relax in
God's love, allowing it to envelop your life and your
heart. Then follow him. Never, never, never quit.

Gardeners know that raising flowers takes patience.
Growing to maturity in God also requires patience—from
God and from you. But rest assured—it is worth it.

*Love never stops being patient,
never stops believing, never stops
hoping, never gives up.*

1 Corinthians 13:7 GOD'S WORD

A WARM AND FUZZY HUG

For you who welcome him, in whom he dwells—even though you still experience all the limitations of sin— you yourself experience life on God's terms.
ROMANS 8:10 MSG

People have a daily quotient of hugs and touches they need to feel loved and affirmed. Hugs are more

than wrapping your arms around another person. Hugs also are found in the smiles of loved ones, in the sentiments of greeting cards, and in the comfort and coziness of favorite sweaters.

Hugs are an emotional bond. God hugs you with his words of love in the Bible, with a melody that touches your heart, and even with a sunrise that takes your breath away. God has made this world as a demonstration of his love for you. Enjoy being in God's presence today.

God, allow me to relax in your presence, to lean my head on your chest, and to hear your heartbeat of love for me.
AMEN.

We have seen the hand of
God at work today.

Luke 7:16 NLT

AGAINST ALL ODDS

With God we shall do valiantly; it is he
who will tread down our foes.

PSALM 60:12 ESV

God told Gideon to assemble an army, and he gathered 30,000 men. Messengers brought back word  that the enemy outnumbered them, and Gideon was concerned. But God told Gideon to reduce the number of men; he said this not once but three times, until only 300 men were left to fight.

Gideon realized that he and his men were not going to win the fight—God was. No matter how big the attack in your life looks, and no matter how fierce the fight seems, God is the one who wins the battles. Place your trust in him, and you will always come out a winner—no matter the odds.

God, I place all the battles in my life in your hands. I
trust you to lead me where you would have me go.
AMEN.

Teach me to do Your will, for You are my God; Your Spirit is good. Lead me in the land of uprightness.

Psalm 143:10 NKJV

NO MORE SECRETS

I will show my greatness and my holiness, and I will make myself known in the sight of many nations. Then they will know that I am the Lord.

EZEKIEL 38:23 NIV

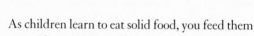

As children learn to eat solid food, you feed them in stages. If you tried to feed newborns steak, they wouldn't be able to digest it. Once they get the taste for other new foods, however, it's a joy to see them want more and more.

God feeds you his truths in the same way. He doesn't reveal all of himself to you at one time; he teaches you in smaller morsels, allowing you time to digest his truths. The more he gives you, the more you want. He rejoices over each step of progress you make in feeding from the Bible.

Just as God lets you grow in him in small bites and small steps, allow others to grow in him at their own pace too.

Solid food is for mature people who have been trained to know right from wrong.

Hebrews 5:14 CEV

HOLY ANOINTING

You shall also consecrate them, that they may be most holy; whatever touches them shall be holy.

EXODUS 30:29 NASB

"Safe!" the umpire shouts as the runner slides into home just ahead of the catcher's glove. The runner is thrilled; he just scored a run.

The catcher isn't so happy; he was sure the runner was out. The catcher argues with the umpire, to no avail. What he says goes. Even if he's wrong.

How comforting to serve a God who is never wrong. God's touch on your life imparts his characteristics, and he wants you to pass that touch along. When God shows you love, show it to someone who is unlovable. When God shows you mercy, pass some mercy along to one who needs it.

God is seen in the way your life touches others. You can show God to the world through your words, your actions, and your lifestyle.

You must follow my example, as
I follow the example of Christ.

1 Corinthians 11:1 CEV

FINDING THE ANSWER

I will show myself holy among those who are near me. I will be glorified before all the people.
LEVITICUS 10:3 NLT

When you watch children playing hide-and-seek, you will notice there are one or two favorite

places where children choose to hide. It's interesting to watch the seeker wandering around in puzzlement while looking for the hiders.

God doesn't play hide-and-seek with you. He's right there with you. He designed you to

have an intimate relationship with him. He shows himself clearly in the Bible, and he shows himself to others through you and the way you live. You show God's presence in your life by glorifying him.

Spending time with God creates an intimate relationship with him that will spill over into all areas of your life. That relationship will then change others.

With God we will gain the victory, and he will trample down our enemies.

Psalm 108:13 NIV

KEEPING YOUR FOCUS

*Depart from me, evildoers, that I may observe the
commandments of my God.*
PSALM 119:115 NASB

When a duckling hatches, it bonds with the first
moving object it sees, normally the mother duck.
However, if the first moving
object is the farmer in a pair of
green rubber boots, the duckling
bonds with the boots instead and
follows them everywhere.

God desires you to bond
with him as well. When you are
convinced that he has your best
interests at heart, you won't question where he leads.
At times the path may seem narrow, but it is never
crooked. While all around you there may be danger,
if you follow God you will always be safe.

*God created ducklings to bond with their mother because
that's the safest place for them. The safest place for you is
under God's protection.*

He will spread his wings over you and keep you secure. His faithfulness is like a shield or a city wall.

Psalm 91:4 CEV

JOY IN THE NIGHT

"In those days, at that time," declares the LORD, "the people of Israel and the people of Judah together will go in tears to seek the LORD their God."

JEREMIAH 50:4 NIV

A light, warning of danger ahead, shines across the water. Sailors could choose to be afraid of the lighthouse; wherever there is a lighthouse, there is  danger of running aground. But sailors know the lighthouse is for their protection.

Rest assured that God's presence is a friend to you. God warns you of dangers ahead and lets you know if you're getting off course. These warnings bring you the assurance of a God who wants what's best for you. After coming through a storm in your life, you'll find the path ahead clear and well lit. Ask God for his presence in your life—he's waiting to hear from you.

God, I know that sometimes I run from you, when I should be running to you. Let me feel your presence here, now. Let me see your face.
AMEN.

*You, the LORD God, keep my lamp
burning and turn darkness to light.*

Psalm 18:28 CEV

FRIENDS AGAIN

He has now reconciled you in His fleshly body through death, in order to present you before Him holy and blameless and beyond reproach.

<small>COLOSSIANS 1:22 NASB</small>

Remember your childhood, when the simplest disagreement resulted in broken friendship? But when you realized how much you nearly lost, it was  easy to put aside pride, in the name of harmony.

God has already made provision for settling differences in your life. He used his son's life to show you how to live a life that's pleasing to him. He used his son's death to illustrate that if you give your life to him you will be with him forever. Choose to live life on his terms, because that's the best place to be. Friends of God. That has a nice sound to it.

God, since you are my friend, I know you want what's best for me. Help me to give up what I want for what you want.
AMEN.

Just as lotions and fragrance give sensual delight, a sweet friendship refreshes the soul.

Proverbs 27:9 MSG

A HIGHER STANDARD

Judge me by your righteousness, O LORD my God.
PSALM 35:24 GOD'S WORD

When you were a child, you did what your parents said to do, such as say your prayers and go to bed at a certain time. And when you were away from your  parents, you probably stayed up late. Soon you learned that if you didn't get enough sleep you'd be tired the next day.

Living in God's presence also requires choices. Your choices are reflected in your life and in your relationship with him. Just as when you were younger, reevaluate your priorities and see if you need to make some changes. Choose to be refreshed in God today. Choose to live a life pleasing to God.

God, when I get ahead of you and look to please only me,
remind me that I belong to you.
AMEN.

Hear my prayer, O God; listen to the words of my mouth.

Psalm 54:2 NIV

THE JOY OF ADOPTION

Once you're convinced that he is right and righteous,
you'll recognize that all who practice
righteousness are God's true children.

1 JOHN 2:29 MSG

When you walk in the door on Adoption Day at
the local animal shelter, the first thing you hear is the

sound of barking dogs. Many
of those dogs will go home
that day; they will be chosen
by people who really want
those particular dogs for their
very own.

Being in God's family is
as exciting as being chosen on Adoption Day. God
searched the world until he found you. He has great
plans for you, even more so than those new owners
have for their chosen "fur" babies. He made special
plans to include you in his family. Let God know you
love being with him and that you're so very happy
that he chose you.

God, thank you for choosing me. I pray that
my life will be a constant song of praise
to you for bringing me into your family.
AMEN.

*His Holy Spirit speaks to us deep
in our hearts and tells us that
we are God's children.*

Romans 8:16 NLT

IT'S NOT ABOUT RELIGION

I am the LORD who makes you holy.
EXODUS 31:13 GOD'S WORD

Two sisters were playing a game, with the older explaining the rules to the younger. When the younger child objected that it was too complicated, her sister again patiently explained the rules. Finally, the younger one stood up and declared, "I'm not playing anymore. There are too many rules!"

As you draw close to God, well-meaning friends might give you a list of rules and regulations you must follow. All the rules in the world won't bring you closer to God. Do the right thing because of your relationship with God. Let God examine your heart, and toss away the religion. Let an intimate relationship with him be the essence of your life.

An essence is achieved by removing all other ingredients. Make God the essence of your life by choosing him above all else.

*Real religion, the kind that passes
muster before God the Father, is this:
Reach out to the homeless and loveless
in their plight, and guard against
corruption from the godless world.*

James 1:27 MSG

THE HERITAGE OF GOD

The Olympic Games are often the pinnacle of an athlete's career. The world's best athletes gather  together to compete for gold and honor. A lifetime of training and discipline is concentrated on one event. Winners are separated from second best by milliseconds or fractions of an inch.

God has chosen you because he loves you, not because of your abilities. One stumble or fall doesn't mean you're out of God's grace. When you seek God in your life, you're seeking something far more important than a gold medal. You're seeking the source of all wealth, the Creator of all. He has already determined that you are a winner!

God, thank you that you would use me as an example.
Remind me that others are watching me,
and guide my steps accordingly.
AMEN.

Always set an example by doing good things. When you teach, be an example of moral purity and dignity.

Titus 2:7 GOD'S WORD

SEEKING GOD'S
BLESSINGS

In our spiritual nature, faith causes us to wait eagerly for the confidence that comes with God's approval.

Galatians 5:5 GOD'S WORD

FINDING YOUR WAY

There will be a highway called the Holy Road. No one rude or rebellious is permitted on this road. It's for God's people exclusively—impossible to get lost on this road.
ISAIAH 35:8 MSG

Driving down a dark road at night during a snowstorm isn't a pleasant experience. Landmarks

are hidden behind the dark and the snow, and it's easy to get lost. Sometimes the only way you know you're on the road is to follow the tire tracks of the car ahead of you.

In direct contrast, God's way is clear and direct. One method he uses to show you his way is the Bible. In it he tells you exactly what to do and where to go to reach your final destination—heaven. God has given you a map so you won't get lost or delayed. Read, memorize, and remind yourself of his directions every day.

God posts many No Trespassing signs for your protection to point you back to the main road and to get you where you're going.

Because I love your commands more than gold, more than pure gold, and because I consider all your precepts right, I hate every wrong path.

Psalm 119:127–128 NIV

REACHING FOR THE SUN

You protected me from death and kept me from
stumbling, so that I would please you and
follow the light that leads to life.
PSALM 56:13 CEV

Few living things can survive without sunlight.
Green plants use sunlight to produce energy for
 growth. Animals convert sun-
light into essential vitamins
and amino acids. Longer days
of sunshine produce seeds and
fruit. Shorter days produce
hibernation and conservation
of resources.

God created the sun to provide the earth with
what it needs to survive. He created an innate longing
in you to walk in sunlight as a reflection of his love for
you. There is a God-shaped emptiness in you that
only God can fill. Being in God's presence will cause
you to produce spiritual fruit that will draw others to
God.

God, only in you can I be fulfilled and filled full.
Let me feel your love for me in everything I do.
AMEN.

Every single good
promise that the Lord had given
the nation of Israel came true.

JOSHUA 21:45 GOD'S WORD

HIS VERY OWN

*You are a holy people to the Lord your God; the Lord
your God has chosen you to be a people for
Himself, a special treasure above all the
peoples on the face of the earth.*

DEUTERONOMY 7:6 NKJV

When pirates roamed the oceans stealing gold
and valuables from ships, people lived in fear. Many

pirates buried their treasure
on deserted islands with the
intention of going back for it
later. Much of this treasure
has never been recovered.

You are God's precious
silver and gold. He values
you above anything else he has created. He doesn't
bury you or hide you away where no one else can see
you. Instead, he shows you off to the world. "Here's
my wealth!" he shouts to the nations as he proudly
holds you high in his hands. You are God's gift to the
world.

*Buried treasure can't make a difference; it can't buy food
or clothing or heal the sick. God chooses to use you to
show others the love of God.*

*How much better it is to get wisdom
than gold! And to get understanding is
to be chosen above silver.*

Proverbs 16:16 NASB

WE'RE HAVING A PARTY!

There you shall eat before the Lord your God, and you shall rejoice, you and your households, in all that you undertake, in which the Lord your God has blessed you.
DEUTERONOMY 12:7 ESV

The invitation reads, "Come to the party. Have fun. Eat lots of good food. Meet nice people." It's nice  to be invited to a party where you don't have to do all the work.

This isn't just another ordinary party. This is God's party for you. He puts on the best celebrations. In God, there is no end to what he has in store to give you. And the party never has to end with him. Accept the invitation. Call and let him know you wouldn't miss this one for the world.

Bountiful God, thank you for giving me so much every day. Thank you that in you there is no end to the celebration.
AMEN.

*They will celebrate your abundant
goodness and joyfully sing
of your righteousness.*

Psalm 145:7 NIV

A PLACE OF WORSHIP

*Start with God—the first step in learning
is bowing down to God.*
PROVERBS 1:7 MSG

Easter bonnet. Christmas tree. Thanksgiving
dinner setting. Valentine's heart decorations. Saint
Patrick's Day shamrocks. You take them out once a
year, and then store them
away until the next time.

Worship is not meant to
be relegated to Sunday morn-
ings and then left on a shelf for
the rest of the week. Think of
worship as the gas in your
tank. If you don't fill up with
the fuel of worship, you won't be able to give to others in the form of ministry and relationships. Seek
ways to be in worship at all times. It isn't a physical
activity; it's an attitude of the heart.

*God, show me ways in my life that I can be in
worship with you all the time. Fill me
with the fuel of your presence.*
AMEN.

I urge you, brethren, by the mercies of
God, to present your bodies a living and
holy sacrifice, acceptable to God, which
is your spiritual service of worship.

Romans 12:1 NASB

BUILDING ON A STRONG FOUNDATION

Dedicate your hearts and lives to serving the LORD your God. Start building the holy place of the LORD.
1 CHRONICLES 22:19 GOD'S WORD

When a large building is being built, work seems to sit for months; the future building seems to be little more than a hole in the ground. Then suddenly, con-struction efforts seem to yield hints of what will be; the shapeless mounds begin to look like a real building. In reality, the most important part of the building—the foundation—was being constructed when it looked like no progress was being made.

When it seems that you aren't making much headway in your relationship with God, realize that you're building the foundation. Persevere in building the foundation that will never fail. The Bible is the foundation for your life. God's presence is the cement that holds your life together.

The foundation bears the weight and supports the rest of the building. A strong faith foundation will support you through any storm that comes along.

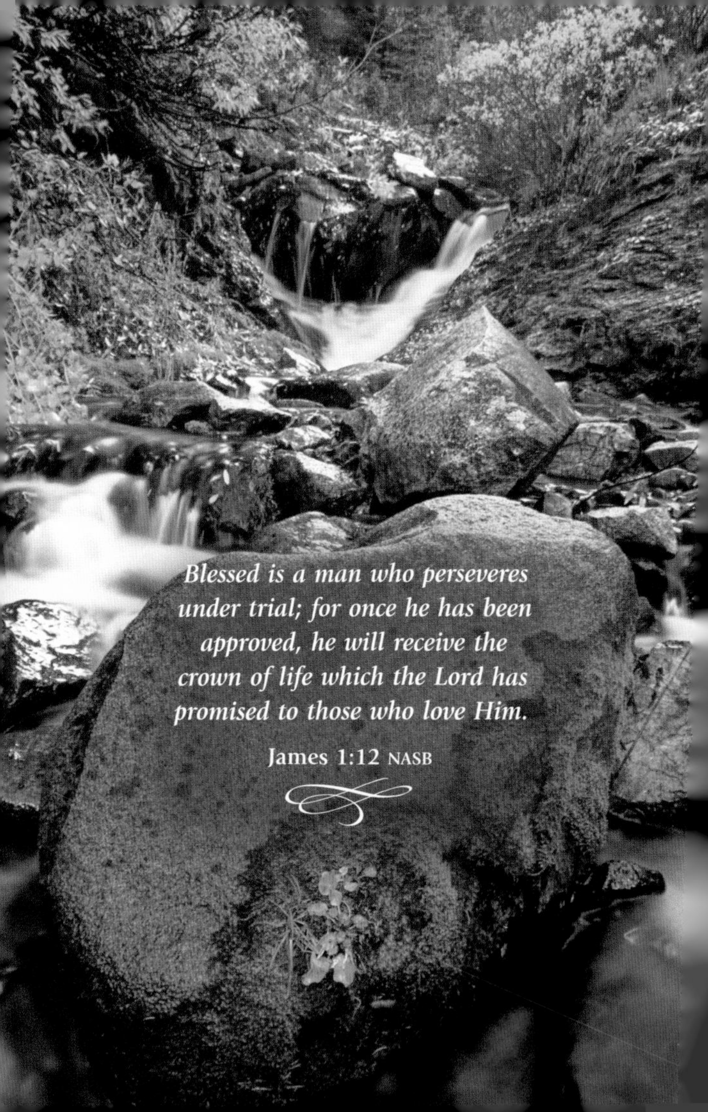

Blessed is a man who perseveres under trial; for once he has been approved, he will receive the crown of life which the Lord has promised to those who love Him.

James 1:12 NASB

CLEAR VISION

*He chose us in him before the creation of the world to
be holy and blameless in his sight.*
 EPHESIANS 1:4 NIV

Your eyes are set in the front of your face so that
you can see what's coming toward you. Animals' eyes

are normally set closer to the
sides of their heads so they can
see what's coming from behind
and from the side. Animals
need to be able to run away;
you need to be able to run to.

God created you to run to
him, not away from him. Run to God by choosing to
be where he is, by doing the things he does. God's eye-
sight is perfect, and he sees the person you are becoming. Run to God today and every day.

*God, guide my steps when I falter in coming to you. Light
my paths. Make me a light to lead others to you.*
AMEN.

You're my place of quiet retreat; I
wait for your Word to renew me.

Psalm 119:114 MSG

A NEW WARDROBE

As those who have been chosen of God, holy and
beloved, put on a heart of compassion, kindness,
humility, gentleness and patience.
COLOSSIANS 3:12 NASB

A little girl was walking with her grandmother
in the park. It was the same route they took every day,

and the little girl was noticing
the trees. At an apple tree, she
stared at the white flowers that
had blossomed overnight.
Finally she spoke, "Grandma,
look! The tree has a new dress
on!"

God dresses his trees in wonderful outfits of
flowers and fruit, and he dresses you in beauty. When
you choose godly attributes such as compassion, kindness, and patience, you draw others to God. Show
others his goodness and mercy for them. He is waiting to clothe you in all his beauty.

Merciful God, clothe me today in your righteousness.
When others look at me, let them see only you.
AMEN.

I will clothe her priests
with salvation, and
her saints will ever
sing for joy.

Psalm 132:16 NIV

HONESTY

*I know, my God, that you test the heart and
have pleasure in uprightness.*
1 CHRONICLES 29:17 ESV

Have you ever bitten into a shiny red apple and
found it to be rotten to the core? You can't always tell

the quality of a thing by what it
looks like. Even that dusty old
dresser in the attic could be a
priceless antique.

God doesn't look at your
physical surface either. His pri-
ority isn't how you look or what
you wear. God cares about your
heart. He sees not only the good
deeds you do, the hours you volunteer, and how well
you treat your elderly parents, but he cares about
more than your actions. He's looking at the changes
inside, not outside, you. When you fashion your life
around God, nothing else matters to him.

*Giving your life to God is not a one-time decision—it's
an ongoing work every minute of every day.
Commitment shows God who you are.*

May all who search for you be filled with joy and gladness.

Psalm 70:4 NLT

ALL GROWN-UP

Run after mature righteousness—faith, love,
peace—joining those who are in honest
and serious prayer before God.
2 TIMOTHY 2:22 MSG

In the animal world, babies are fed, protected, nurtured, and trained to be what their parents are. Horses raise baby horses, and birds raise baby birds.

When you first begin to believe the promises of God, you need feeding, protection, and training to become more confident in who you are in Christ. Just as a mother horse raises her foal so it can then raise its own, God brings you to spiritual maturity so you can go out and help raise others. God doesn't expect you to do this on your own; he uses others who are growing in relationship with him, just as he uses you.

Growth creates hunger. Growth in your relationship
with God will cause you to want more of
him in all areas of your life.

From the very first day you heard and recognized the truth of what God is doing, you've been hungry for more.

Colossians 1:6 MSG

THE CARPENTER'S CREATION

The whole building, being fitted together, grows into a holy temple in the Lord.
EPHESIANS 2:21 NKJV

Longer workweeks have resulted in a serious attitude toward rest and relaxation. As a result, as more and more people seek a sanctuary away from the office, vacation home and recreational vehicle sales have skyrocketed over the last decade.

Your relationship with God is a place of respite away from the demands of life. As you come into his presence, as you seek more and more of him on a regular basis, you will find an easing of the burdens of the day. Spending time with God creates an inner peace that comes only from him. Retreat into that safe haven often. It's a refuge, created especially for you.

Unlike a vacation cottage that can get blown down by a storm, your sanctuary with God can withstand any assault.

He said to them, "Why are you afraid, O you of little faith?" Then he rose and rebuked the winds and the sea, and there was a great calm.

Matthew 8:26 ESV

UNDER HIS WINGS

Let me dwell in Your tent forever; let me take
refuge in the shelter of Your wings.
PSALM 61:4 NASB

No matter how hard the firefighter tried, the kitten wouldn't come out of the drainpipe. Finally, the

firefighter went to the opposite end of the pipe and opened the nozzle on his fire hose, pouring a controlled flow of water down the pipe. The kitten shot out the other end, into the waiting arms of its owner.

The firefighter wasn't trying to drown the kitten; he was encouraging it to go in the right direction. Sometimes God will do that with you too. When you feel that you're backed into a corner, don't run from God. Allow God to flood you with his love for you. In him is a refuge and safety beyond what the world can offer.

God, when I just don't get it, remind me that you have my
best interests at heart. Let your presence rain down on me.
AMEN.

God, you're my refuge. I trust in you and I'm safe!

Psalm 91:2 MSG

LIKE A ROCK

You yourselves like living stones are being built up as a
spiritual house, to be a holy priesthood.
1 PETER 2:5 ESV

In the Old Testament, only priests had a relationship with God that consisted of laws, traditions, and

rituals, rigorously carried out. The high priest was permitted to go into God's presence only once a year.

God knew the people weren't ready for a one-on-one relationship with him, and so he appointed priests to intercede for them. With Jesus, however, God opened the way for you to have a personal relationship with him. God is building you into a priest, and he is inviting you into his presence. Go into God's presence daily, and show others how to do the same.

Living in God's presence is claiming your heritage—a
holy priesthood. But don't just claim it—make a
difference in the lives of others with it.

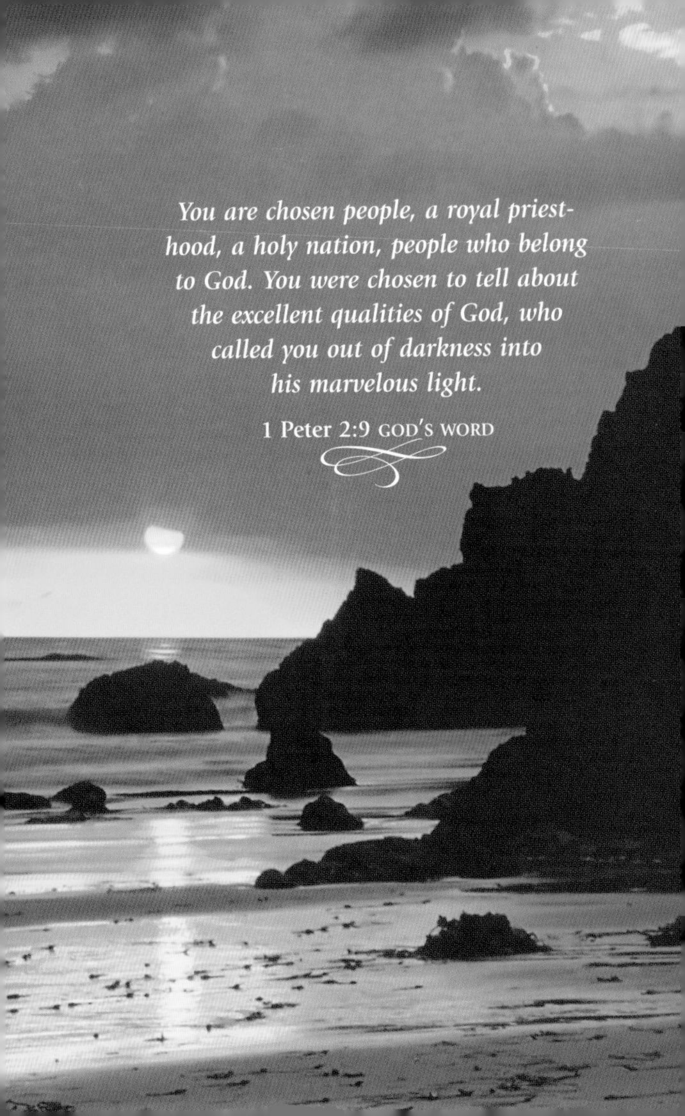

You are chosen people, a royal priesthood, a holy nation, people who belong to God. You were chosen to tell about the excellent qualities of God, who called you out of darkness into his marvelous light.

1 Peter 2:9 GOD'S WORD

A LIGHT IN THE DARK

*You shall seek the Lord at the place which the
Lord your God will choose from all your tribes,
to establish His name there for His dwelling,
and there you shall come.*

DEUTERONOMY 12:5 NASB

At night, away from the lights of the city, the
stars are incredibly bright. Undistracted by other

lights, you can see the stars
shine across the miles, each
one numbered and named by
God.

God put you here to be a
light in the dark. Be his
dwelling, the place where his
spirit resides. You are very
important to his plan, to light the way for the world.
There are others who are floundering around in the
dark as you once were. Reach out to them, by showing them God's presence in your life.

*When you feel insignificant, remember that the sun is a
small star that seems bright because of its closeness to the
earth. Be a light in the dark for others.*

I, the Lord, have called You in righteousness, and will hold Your hand; I will keep You and give You as a covenant to the people, as a light to the Gentiles.

Isaiah 42:6 NKJV

SEEKING GOD'S
DIRECTION

If you look for me in earnest, you will find me when you seek me.

Jeremiah 29:13 NLT

GIVING ALL YOU HAVE

*We have been set apart as holy because Jesus
Christ did what God wanted him to do by
sacrificing his body once and for all.*
HEBREWS 10:10 GOD'S WORD

The lieutenant knew that this was a dangerous
mission and that some of his men wouldn't be coming
back. He thought of his wife and two small boys, safe
at home. Because of what he
and the others were doing, his
family, and many more, were
safe.

Every day, hard orders
are given and obeyed. Jesus
chose to live his life doing
what God the Father asked him to do. When you put
aside your wants and desires and replace them with
God's plan for your life, you will be showing others
how to do the same. Every day, choose to give God all
you have.

*God, search my heart, take out anything that isn't from
you, and replace it with your will for my life.*
AMEN.

O LORD, *You have searched me and known me.*

Psalm 139:1 NASB

A SHOWER A DAY

Husbands, love your wives, as Christ loved the church and gave himself up for her, that he might sanctify her, having cleansed her by the washing of water with the word.
EPHESIANS 5:25–26 ESV

Approximately three quarters of the earth's surface is covered by water. Water is used for many purposes—drinking, washing, and irrigation among them. It's also used for transportation, fertilization,  recreation, and even for religious ceremonies.

Water is used for baptism, a symbol of your unity in Christ and of your being cleansed. When you partake of the life and freedom that Jesus offers, he promises you will not thirst for the things of this world. Jesus' selfless act of sacrifice makes you clean from the past and rehydrates your soul for the things to come. Drink deeply of him.

God, give me a thirst for more of you in my life. Cleanse me with your word, and set me apart for your use.
AMEN.

*Cleanse me with hyssop,
and I will be clean;
wash me, and I will
be whiter than snow.*

Psalm 51:7 NIV

SET APART FOR GOD

It is God's will that you should be sanctified.
1 THESSALONIANS 4:3 NIV

Her fingers carefully peeled back the tape on the package. Inside was a pretty new nightgown. She set

the package aside. "I'll just save that for good," she said. It would go into the dresser along with the other nightgowns being saved "for good," never to be used.

God doesn't change you from the inside out so that he can set you on a shelf or in a dresser drawer, never to be used. Instead, he equips you and sends you into the world to make a difference. You can't help change the lives of others unless you get into their lives. Take that step of faith today.

Even when it might not look like it to you, God is working on your life so that you can help others to make changes in their lives.

You love justice and hate evil. And so,
your God chose you and made you
happier than any of your friends.

Psalm 45:7 CEV

THE BEST PLACE TO BE

*Day and night I'll stick with GOD; I've got a good thing
going and I'm not letting go.*
PSALM 16:8 MSG

When you venture into unknown territory, it's
nice to have something around you that is familiar.

Whether it be a trusted friend, a
map, a note with the directions
written on it—it doesn't really
matter, as long as there is some
reference point.

Walking with God often
takes you into strange territory.
He leads you to places and situations where you've never been
before. God is your trusted friend who has never
failed you and never will. The Bible is a road map for
you, the directions on the right way to go. His path is
sure and straight, and he has lit the way for you.

*The Bible is like a self-perpetuating battery for your
light—the more you use it, the stronger it becomes.
Use it often to direct your path.*

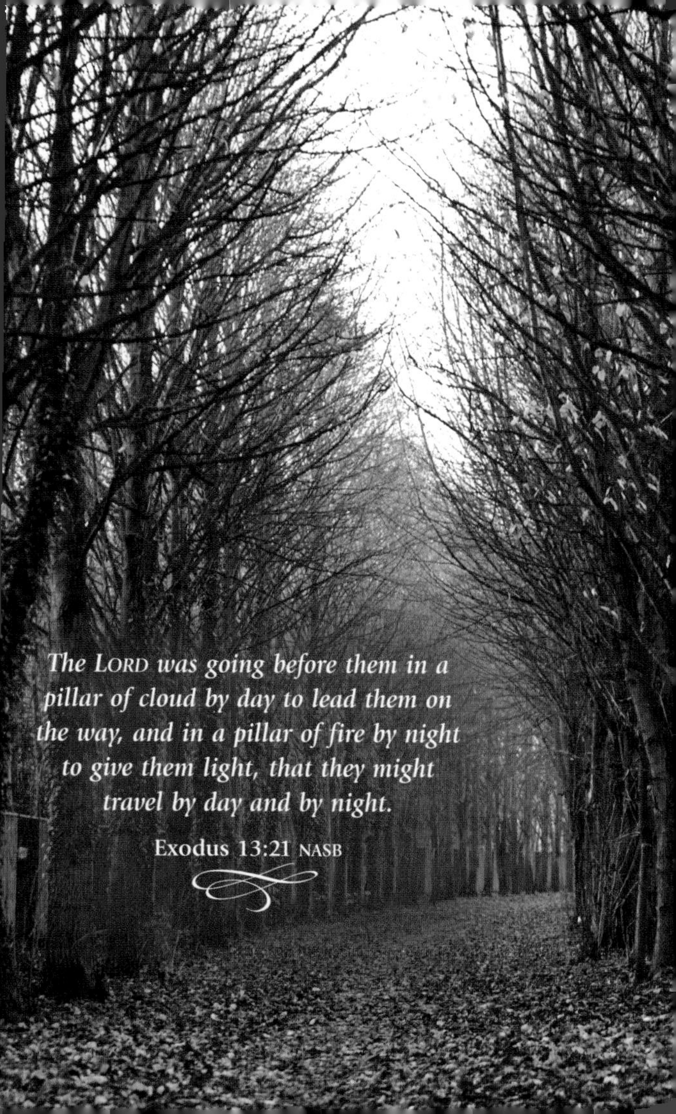

The LORD was going before them in a pillar of cloud by day to lead them on the way, and in a pillar of fire by night to give them light, that they might travel by day and by night.

Exodus 13:21 NASB

PLEASED TO SAVE

Be pleased, O LORD, to save me;
O LORD, come quickly to help me.
PSALM 40:13 NIV

The children laugh as they dodge "it." Running as fast as they can, they head for home, where they're

safe. Sometimes one of them stumbles just inches from home and becomes "it" for the next round.

God is home for his children, a place of safety. You always feel that safety envelop you as you come into God's refuge. He knew there would be battles to fight, and that sometimes you'd get tired and need to rest. His presence is that safe place, and you don't have to worry about stumbling just short of safety. He is there to pick you up and bring you home.

Living all the time in God's presence is the safest place to be. Run to him all the time, not just when you are tired.

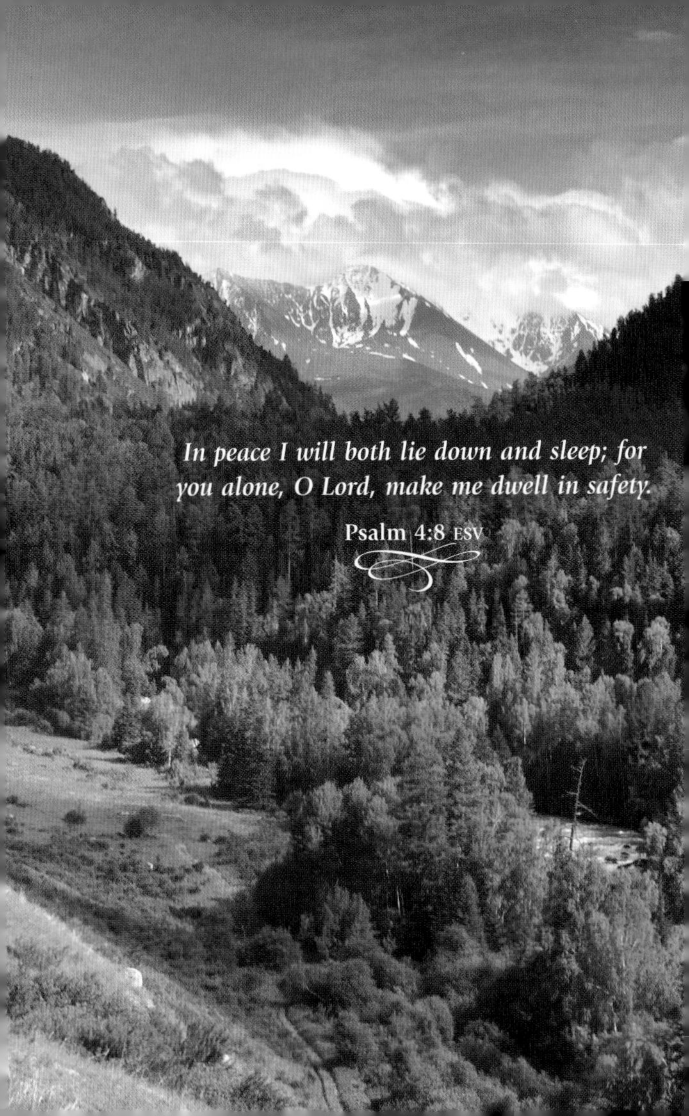

In peace I will both lie down and sleep; for you alone, O Lord, make me dwell in safety.

Psalm 4:8 ESV

A SAFE PLACE TO GO

*Be to me a rock of habitation to which I may
continually come; You have given commandment to
save me, for You are my rock and my fortress.*
PSALM 71:3 NASB

The sand castles glistened as the setting sun reflected off the water. Earlier in the day, thousands of people had gathered to watch the castle building contest. Now, the high tide crept toward the structures.

God's refuge is invincible and eternal. No waves or storms can tear down what God has built up. And that includes you. When you don't know where else to turn, turn to God. Come into his castle so you can go out into the world, a strong fortress of the Living God. You might be someone else's refuge tomorrow.

*Holy God, remind me that this work you are
doing in me isn't just for me. It's also for
others, who also need a safe place.*
AMEN.

You hold me safe beyond the reach of my enemies; you save me from violent opponents.

Psalm 18:48 NLT

ONE ON ONE IN A CROWD

Moses brought the people out of the camp to meet with God, and they stood at the foot of the mountain.
EXODUS 19:17 NKJV

Mob mentality. It's when an emotion begun with one spreads to more, and then a large group of people acts in one accord. Many times, the individuals in the

group don't know the reason behind their actions—they're just going along with the rest.

Sometimes, corporate worship can look and feel like that. You do what the rest of the congregation is doing, no matter how you really feel. God is interested in where your heart is, not what your body is doing. Worship is where you meet with God, and it doesn't matter if you're one or one in a thousand. Meet with God today, one on one, even in a crowd.

Meeting with God in corporate worship benefits the whole group. Feel free to worship God as he leads and not as the crowd leads.

David, wearing a linen ephod, danced before the LORD with all his might.

2 Samuel 6:14 NIV

COUNT YOUR BLESSINGS

*When they see their many children and
material blessings, they will recognize
the holiness of the Holy One of Israel.*

ISAIAH 29:23 NLT

When the sun shines brightly, when the world is
as it should be, and when things just seem to go right,
it's easy to be thankful to God and
sing praises to his name because of
his blessings and abundance.

But it's especially important
to praise God for his blessings
when things don't seem to be
going so well. The praise reminds
you that even when it doesn't look
like it, God is in control. He gives
because he is holy, not because you ask. He gives
because of his promises, not because you need it.
Remind yourself today how good God is—and stand
back and watch the blessings pour in.

*God, many times my prayer life consists of asking for
needs to be met. In truth, the only real need I have is you.*
AMEN.

I pray to you, Lord. So when the time is right, answer me and help me with your wonderful love.

Psalm 69:13 CEV

WHEN YOU MEAN WELL

*He was well-intentioned—his heart was in the
right place, in tune with God.*
1 Kings 15:14 msg

The five-year-old made his way to where his
mother lay sleeping. He whispered her name, balanc-ing the tray carefully. She opened
her eyes, smiled at him, and saw
the tray. Burned toast, milk in a
plastic cup spilling onto the place-
mat, soggy cereal. Happy Mother's
Day. Her small son had done his
best and had then tried to clean up
the mess.

Sound like your walk with God sometimes? No
matter how hard you try, you mess up. God looks at
the intentions of your heart, not the outcome. God is
your biggest fan. He is encouraging you on, so get up
and try again.

*Never be afraid of failure with God. Instead, look
for ways to show him how much you love him.
Demonstrate your love by doing your best.*

*Examine me, O LORD, and test me. Look
closely into my heart and mind.*

Psalm 26:2 GOD'S WORD

WATCHING AND WAITING

*Because you trusted me, I will preserve
your life and keep you safe.*
JEREMIAH 39:18 NLT

When you take a cruise, you will notice lifeboats
on the ship. They are there in case there is an emer-
gency, and you have to aban-
don ship. And even though
the captain knows about the
lifeboats too, he still sails carefully, to keep you safe.

God doesn't have life-
boats that you can jump into
when dangers come. Instead,
he preserves your life in other ways. God has promised that because you trust him, he will not only lead
you to a place of safety, he will also keep you safe.
Trust in God and his promises to bring you safely to
your destination—him.

*God knows you're safe in him, and he shows you so you
can know it too. You can relax and enjoy the trip.*

Be like those who stay the course with committed faith and then get everything promised to them.

Hebrews 6:12 MSG

THE MEMORY BOOK

You will be remembered before the Lord your God, and
you will be saved from your enemies.
NUMBERS 10:9 NKJV

Where photo albums and genealogy records left off, memory books have picked up. Memory books combine photos and other memorabilia with stickers and decorations to commemorate and immortalize an occasion, event, or even a lifetime.

God's memory book is the Book of Life. In it he records your name as one who chose to follow him, to include him in your life, and to teach others to do the same. You do that in the big things in your life, like how you raise your kids, and in the small things that you don't even know others are watching, like how you treat the cashier at the store.

God, the thought of you brings a smile to my face.
Remind me to make you smile often
and to share my joy with others.
AMEN.

When they were discouraged, I smiled at them. My look of approval was precious to them.

Job 29:24 NLT

HEART AND SOUL

Seek the LORD your God and you will find him,
if you search after him with all your
heart and with all your soul.
DEUTERONOMY 4:29 ESV

The rescue team fanned out along the search grid, desperately looking for signs of the missing child  who had wandered off. Anxious parents called the little girl's name. Up on a nearby hill, a wolf was howling at the moon. This wasn't a safe place for a four-year-old child to be lost.

Being alone in this world is not a safe place for you either. There are many distractions and temptations, seemingly innocent incidents, leading to possible disaster. When you find yourself wandering away from God, don't keep running. Stop, pray, and wait for God. He's out there looking for you right now.

If you get lost, stop and watch. Trying to find your
way back will only get you more lost. You are
easier to find if you stay in one place.

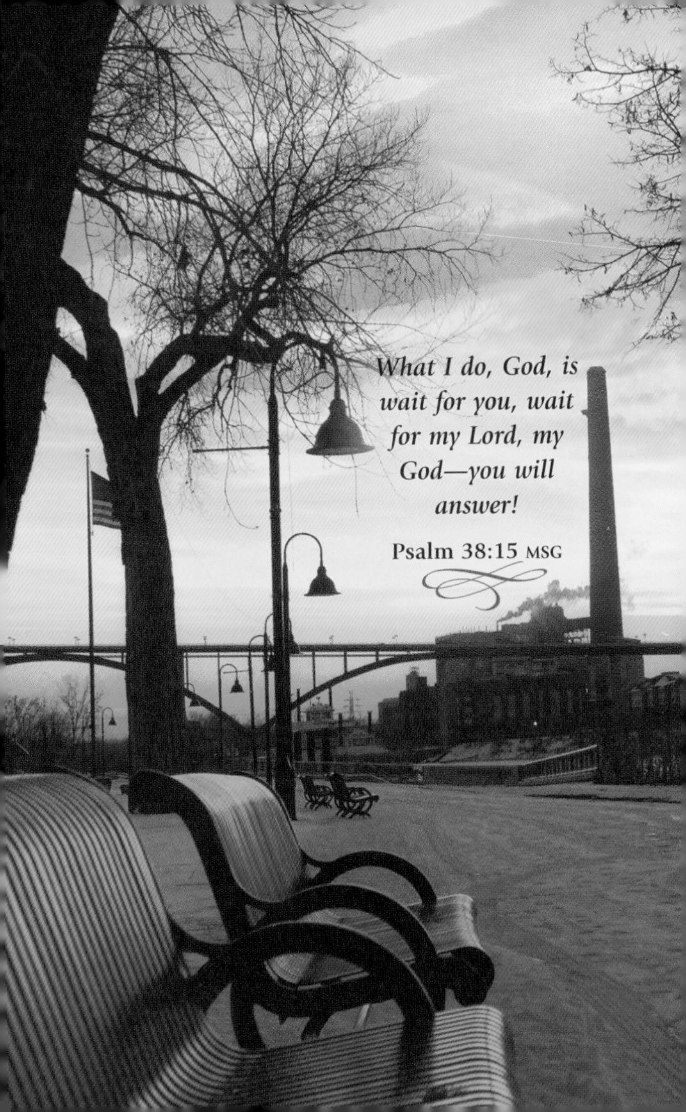

What I do, God, is wait for you, wait for my Lord, my God—you will answer!

Psalm 38:15 MSG

SAFE AND SECURE

*My people will live in a peaceful habitation, and in
secure dwellings and in undisturbed resting places.*
ISAIAH 32:18 NASB

Eagles build their nests up high in order to protect their young from predators and so that the eaglets

can learn to fly. If the eaglets don't
learn to fly the first time they're
pushed from the nest, the parent
is quick to catch them before they
hit the ground.

Living in God's presence can
feel so secure that you might not
want to venture out into the
world. But God is training you up to take his message
to the world. The most important part of his message
is that you can live in God's presence while living in
the world. Go, and live the life you were created to
live.

*Gracious God, I want to take your message
to those around me, so that they, too,
can live the life you created them for.*
AMEN.

In the same way that you gave me a
mission in the world, I give them
a mission in the world.

John 17:18 MSG

LIFTED UP

*You rescue me from violent people. That is why I will
give thanks to you, O LORD, among the nations
and make music to praise your name.*
PSALM 18:48–49 GOD'S WORD

David wrote about praise while he was hiding
from Saul, who'd vowed to kill him. David praised

God for all he'd done in David's
life. He reminded himself of God's
promises to him, and of how he'd
been delivered in the past. He con-
cluded by claiming victory, now
and in the future.

You've probably never had to
run for fear of your life. But you've
faced some battles. Some you won,
and some you could've done better.
God never takes you into a battle unless he knows you
can win. Praise God today for all he's brought you
through, for all you're going through now, and for the
victories to come.

*When the victory seems far off and the battle too
big for you, remember the mighty God you
serve. Nothing is too big for God.*

See what I've given you? Safe passage as you walk on snakes and scorpions, and protection from every assault of the Enemy. No one can put a hand on you.

Luke 10:19 MSG

SEEKING GOD'S SAFETY

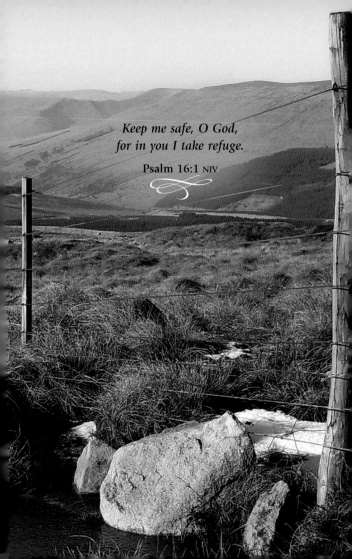

Keep me safe, O God,
for in you I take refuge.

Psalm 16:1 NIV

SAVED FROM DESTRUCTION

He delivered me from my strong enemy, from those who hated me, for they were too strong for me.

PSALM 18:17 NKJV

The young boxer stepped into the ring for his first professional fight. Round after round, the rookie

withstood the assault of the older boxer. The crowd was awestruck at this youngster's determination to win in the face of a stronger and more experienced enemy.

God knows that the enemy is stronger than you are. He knows that without him you don't stand a chance. Like this young boxer, the battles you fight will take you out of your league. But with God on your side, the victory is yours. Take God with you into every battle. God is the one who is stronger than your enemy.

All Powerful God, I know that without you I can do nothing. My only desire is to be where you are.
AMEN.

We are human, but we don't wage war with human plans and methods. We use God's mighty weapons, not mere worldly weapons, to knock down the Devil's strongholds.

2 Corinthians 10:3–4 NLT

LOOKING FOR THE ANSWER

When they were in trouble and got serious, and decided to seek God, the God of Israel, God let himself be found.
2 CHRONICLES 15:4 MSG

The essay was due tomorrow, and she hadn't even started it. It accounted for fifty percent of her grade, so handing it in on time was crucial. But she'd kept putting it off, thinking there was always time. And now time was running out.

You probably don't have a term paper on your list of things undone. But you likely have other uncompleted tasks. That phone call to a friend, that strained relationship that could be repaired, that long overdue letter. Touch base with God; renew your strength before you head off to tie up those loose ends in your life. His presence will be like a refreshing balm to your spirit.

Guilt comes from the enemy as he seeks to destroy your faith by reminding you of your failures. God sees past your failings and into your future.

Those who are believers in Christ Jesus can no longer be condemned.

Romans 8:1 GOD'S WORD

LIVING IN PEACE

Whoever confesses that Jesus is the Son of God,
God abides in him, and he in God.
1 JOHN 4:15 NASB

The puppy felt a slight pain around his neck every time he left the yard area. His owner had set up  an electronic fence and was teaching the dog not to go outside the limits of their property for the puppy's safety and well-being.

God has boundaries that protect you and give you guidelines in which to operate. Living within these boundaries means that you fashion your behavior to conform to the parameters God has set out. Inside the boundaries, you are safe. Step outside, and you may not be. Will stepping outside always get you into trouble? No, but God knows you are better off inside—in his presence.

When you freely choose to live in God's presence, you
find that the protection he offers is not restrictive;
rather, his protection is liberating.

Preserve my life according to your love,
and I will obey the statutes of your mouth.

Psalm 119:88 NIV

NEIGHBORHOOD WATCH

Only those who live by faith are acceptable to me.
HABAKKUK 2:4 CEV

The Guardian Angels are a self-appointed neighborhood watch team that operates in many cities, making neighborhoods safer for residents. Comprising interested citizens, the volunteer groups

patrol the streets at night, deterring crime merely by their presence.

God's presence is also a place of safety. You can be assured that where he is, the enemy isn't. When you trust God to have your best interests at heart, then he is able to deflect the attacks that come. His presence is enough to soothe your fears, calm your frustrations, and clear your mind. Where God is, is peace. Seek that peace today, for yourself, and for others around you.

*God, thank you for caring enough about me to
bring me into your presence. Thank you
for the peace that your presence brings me.*
AMEN.

I pray that the Lord, who gives peace, will always bless you with peace. May the Lord be with all of you.

2 Thessalonians 3:16 CEV

FREE TO COME IN

They will receive the LORD's blessing and have right standing with God their savior. They alone may enter God's presence and worship the God of Israel.
PSALM 24:5–6 NLT

In many cities, the zoo and museums have free days, where you can go in without having to pay

admission. These attractions want you to come and enjoy all they have to offer. But sometimes you have to go looking for information about these free days so you can take advantage of them.

Seeking God's presence requires a desire on your part to enjoy all the good things he has to offer you. You must first acknowledge that you aren't experiencing the best of God, and then decide he is the only one who can give it to you. Enjoy what God is offering today— you belong in his presence.

For information on free days in your city, check the Internet. Each attraction should have a listing or a contact number to call.

This is the gate of the LORD through
which the righteous may enter.

Psalm 118:20 NIV

REJOICE IN PEACE

*You shall offer peace offerings, and shall eat there,
and rejoice before the Lord your God.*
DEUTERONOMY 27:7 NKJV

The little boy stood watching the canary as it sat on its perch and sang. Finally, he asked his mother,  "Mommy, why does the bird just sing and sing?" "Because he's full of joy, and it needs to come out," she answered him.

What a wonderful thought— to be so full of joy that it spills out in every area of your life. Not just in song, but in actions, attitudes, and even private thoughts. God is joy, and when you're full of him and his presence, that joy will need to come out. Look for ways to let that joy spill over in your life today.

*Holy God, thank you for the joy of being in your
presence. Thank you for filling me with
your joy every day, in every way.*
AMEN.

Do not be grieved, for the joy of the Lord is your strength.

Nehemiah 8:10 ESV

THE FAMILY PHOTO ALBUM

A book of remembrance was written before
Him for those who fear the Lord and
who meditate on His name.
MALACHI 3:16 NKJV

Mother and daughter sat on the sofa, side by side,
leafing through page after page of an old photo album

that was faded with time.
"Who's this?" the daughter
asked, pointing to a particu-
larly old photo. The mother
looked at it, then admitted she
didn't know. The daughter
said, "That's sad, that no one
remembers these people."

How comforting to know
and serve a God who lives forever. He hasn't forgotten even one of his children, and he will not forget
you. Visit with God often, renew your relationship
with him, and make sure your children and grand-
children know who he is by telling them about him.

Eternal God, I want you to be alive to me
here and now. Show me how, every day.
AMEN.

I will cause your name to be remembered throughout every generation. That is why the nations will give thanks to you forever and ever.

Psalm 45:17 GOD'S WORD

ALL THE TIME

This book of the law shall not depart from your mouth,
but you shall meditate on it day and night.
JOSHUA 1:8 NASB

"I'll write you every day!" she vowed to her boyfriend as she left on vacation. She wrote only once,

however, and hardly gave him a thought after that. He didn't notice, though, since he was busy too. They had the best of intentions; they just weren't committed.

When you commit to God that you want him to be in your life, he takes it seriously. When he doesn't hear from you, that doesn't mean your relationship is over. It just means there's more work to be done on your part. Stick close to God—he'll never leave you or forsake you.

A big encouragement to stay committed is to remind
yourself of God's promises for you, his plans for
your future, and your part in that plan.

*Watch yourselves, that you
do not forget the covenant
of the Lord your God which
He made with you.*

Deuteronomy 4:23 NASB

FREE TO LIVE

*Now that you've found you don't have to listen to sin
tell you what to do, and have discovered the delight
of listening to God telling you, what a surprise!
A whole, healed, put-together life right now,
with more and more of life on the way!*

ROMANS 6:22 MSG

The American eagle. A symbol of courage, perseverance, and freedom, it soars on the wind, graceful
in its ballet flight. It flies
free, with no natural enemies to worry about.

You are free in God—
free from fear of death and
abandonment. God's prom-
ises for you are life, and life
more abundantly. You don't
have to succumb to temptation; you are strong in
Christ to resist it. You don't have to be afraid of what
the future holds, because you serve a God who has
good plans for you. When you live in God's presence,
you are free to live as he created you—with him.

*God, thank you for inviting me to live with you,
in freedom, from condemnation and sin.
With you is where I always want to be.*
AMEN.

*Satan accused our people in the presence
of God day and night. Now he
has been thrown out!*

Revelation 12:10 CEV

FIRST THINGS FIRST

Seek first the kingdom of God and his righteousness.
MATTHEW 6:33 ESV

"I wanna go to the park!" she shouted, running circles in excitement. "I wanna see the ducks." Her father watched in amusement.  "Don't you think you should change out of your pajamas first?" he asked. What she wanted to do wasn't wrong; she just had it in the wrong order.

You've chosen to take a huge step to grow your relationship with God. You have an idea in your mind how that should happen. Seek God's plans and ideas by seeking him. Get to know this marvelous God who has a plan for you that is always in the right order because it is his order.

Soldiers must learn to walk in step with each other or they will walk on each other. Adjust your step to stay in step with God.

Now I stroll at leisure with God
in the sunlit fields of life.

Psalm 56:13 MSG

RESTORED TO GREATNESS

*May God be gracious to us and bless us and
make his face shine upon us.*
PSALM 67:1 NIV

She carefully removed the old layers of paint, filled in the dents, and sanded. Then she finished the old table to bring out its grain. When she was done, the table looked brand new. She was pleased to give it a new lease on life.

God works in your life by removing the layers you've put up as a barricade against the world. He works on those rough areas and fills in the holes from previous hurts. Then he lovingly covers you with grace and mercy, bringing you into a restored relationship that shows his glory. Allow God to work on you today to give you a new lease on life.

*God, I may not always like how it feels when you are
working on an area of my life, but I trust you completely.*
AMEN.

The heavens declare the glory of God, and the sky above proclaims his handiwork.

Psalm 19:1 ESV

OPEN ARMS

*Because of Christ and our faith in him, we can
now come fearlessly into God's presence,
assured of his glad welcome.*
EPHESIANS 3:12 NLT

Through the garden gate they ran, arms
stretched out toward the welcoming figures waiting
for them on the veranda. Grandma
and Grandpa, huge smiles on their
faces, watched their two grand-
children, then bent down and
scooped them up in their arms,
hugging them close.

The children knew they were
expected, and the grandparents
had been waiting for them to
arrive with anticipation. That's
how God feels about you, too. He waits patiently for
you to get done with the busyness of the day so that
you can spend time together. Run to his presence
without fear. He is glad to see you again.

*Going into God's presence feels like a big warm
hug. Never be afraid of going to God.
He's waiting with open arms.*

I trust you to save me, Lord God,
and I won't be afraid.

Isaiah 12:2 CEV

A JOYFUL SACRIFICE

I will bring a gift and offer a sacrifice to you, Lord. I will praise your name because you are good.

Psalm 54:6 cev

"I don't want to share!" the toddler declared, pulling her toy out of reach of the child near her. "You

need to learn to share," her mother insisted. "If everyone shares, you get to play with more toys."

Sharing and giving don't come naturally. Ownership is built into human nature. That's why God works so hard to encourage sacrificial giving. He showed us the ultimate example in his son, Jesus, who lived a life of giving. When you offer your life to God, you'll find that the benefits far outweigh the cost. Give to him joyously today; give whatever he asks of you.

Bountiful God, remind me you are my provider.
All I have is because you gave it first.
Show me how to give back to you.
AMEN.

Do not be afraid; I will provide for
you and your little ones.

Genesis 50:21 NASB

LIFE-BRINGING FLOODS

Let righteous people rejoice. Let them celebrate in
God's presence. Let them overflow with joy.
PSALM 68:3 GOD'S WORD

A river delta is a fertile area of land created as a result of the flow of sediment down a river. When the

river overflows its bank, the soil is enriched. Still, it can be hard to see the long-term benefits in what looks like destruction.

God's presence can feel like a flood in your life as it washes away some of the dirt. God always brings more than he asks you to give. Just as flooding always leaves more than it takes, God's presence leaves more of him in your life. Be prepared for God to sweep away some of the old and replace it with his new things for you.

Merciful God, you know everything I feel; you
see every tear and every fear. Remind me that
your presence is cause for celebration.
AMEN.

Create in me a clean heart, O God, and renew a steadfast spirit within me.

Psalm 51:10 NASB

SEEKING GOD'S
FAMILY

All creation anticipates the day when it will join God's children in glorious freedom from death and decay.

Romans 8:21 NLT

THE GOOD NEWS

*The angel answered and said to him, "I am Gabriel,
who stands in the presence of God, and was sent to
speak to you and bring you these glad tidings."*
LUKE 1:19 NKJV

Gabriel was sent to announce John the Baptizer's
birth. John was a messenger bringing glad tidings of
God's love for his people. He told the people that they

needed to prepare for the
coming Messiah.

In the same way, you
bring a message. Your life is
a testimony to the grace and
mercy of God. Others will
be drawn to you by God's
presence in your life, and you can show them how to
develop the same relationship with him. You experience his presence by studying his word, spending time
in fellowship with other believers, and praying.
Someone showed you the gift of salvation. Share that
gift of the good news of the gospel to another.

*God, show me your ways and your plan for me. Show
me how to be a messenger to others, proclaiming
your love for me and for them.*
AMEN.

*I have called upon You, for You will
hear me, O God; incline Your ear
to me, and hear my speech.*

Psalm 17:6 NKJV

HOLD YOUR HEAD HIGH

Let not those who wait for You, O Lord God of hosts,
be ashamed because of me; let not those who seek You
be confounded because of me, O God of Israel.
PSALM 69:6 NKJV

She'd given it all she had in the swim meet; still,
she hadn't finished in the top three. Tears in her eyes,
she pulled herself wearily out

of the pool. Her coach hugged
her close. "I'm so proud of
you," the woman declared.
"You did a great job. Don't
ever be ashamed."

Doing what you know is
right should never cause
shame. You cannot dishonor God by doing what he
asks of you. Living in God's presence will often bring
criticism from others, but never from God. Living in
his presence means you're doing your best to look like
him, and he is always perfect.

Just as toddlers need a hand for balance, God
knows you will need him for support, balance,
and guidance as you walk in his ways.

I have, in fact, the greatest confidence in you. If only you knew how proud I am of you!

2 Corinthians 7:4 MSG

COMING TOGETHER

*Save us, O Lord our God, and gather us from among
the nations, that we may give thanks to your holy
name and glory in your praise.*
PSALM 106:47 ESV

At a weekend conference of Christian teens, over
ten thousand teenagers gathered together to praise

God and to learn how to take
him back to their schools, their
neighborhoods, and their
friends. The time spent in
group praise was integral to
their relationship with God
and to their ability to share
that relationship with others.

God loves to see his people gather together in
worship. He knows that sometimes you need to leave
the battles of this world and come into a place of sanctuary. Gather together today with other believers.
God will be there.

*God is looking for people who will worship him in spite
of your differences, not because of your similarities.*

Where two or three are gathered together in My name, I am there in the midst of them.

Matthew 18:20 NKJV

GLAD TO SING HIS PRAISES

I'm about to burst with song; I can't keep quiet about
you. God, my God, I can't thank you enough.
PSALM 30:12 MSG

The city was rejoicing. The local football team
had won their third championship in a row. Two days
later, the city was a shambles after the celebration got

out of hand and fights broke
out. Then people had to strag-
gle back to their lives. Few
lives were really changed by
the victory and celebration.

God's joy is not short-
lived. Living in a state of
rejoicing changes lives. Living

in God's presence will change your life, as long as you
want it to. Your life gets changed because where God
is, there is peace, freedom, life, and abundance,
because that's what God is. Celebrate God's presence
in your life.

God, I'm so glad you're a part of my life. Thank you
for showing me the true meaning of joy.
Thank you for your blessings.
AMEN.

May my lips overflow with praise,
for you teach me your decrees.

Psalm 119:171 NIV

NOOKS AND CRANNIES

*I have seen you in your sanctuary and
gazed upon your power and glory.*
PSALM 63:2 NLT

When you misplace your keys, you frantically try
to remember where you last saw them. You can
search many corners and crevices before you find

them. Sometimes it seems as if
they have taken on a life of
their own and are purposely
hiding.

What a blessing to know
that God doesn't hide himself
from you. He makes himself
visible all around you, even in those dark areas of your
life where you would just as soon not see him. God is
never lost or misplaced. Seek him today, come into the
sanctuary of his presence, and wonder at a God who
is everywhere.

*Thank you, God, that I need not worry about
losing you, that where you are, there is peace,
and that I am never lost with you.*
AMEN.

I have hidden your word in my heart,
that I might not sin against you.

Psalm 119:11 NLT

BE GLAD

You who seek God, let your heart revive.
PSALM 69:32 NASB

When you have been away on a business trip, it feels good to come home. There's something special about knowing that someone you know and love is

going to be waiting for you when you get home. There is no place quite like home.

Living in God's presence brings that same sense of home-coming. You know that no matter what else happens, there is someone there who knows you and loves you. He delights in being with you as much as you delight in being with him. Living in God's presence is like seeing a familiar face when you get home.

Make your next homecoming extra special.
Bring a thank-you gift for the person
meeting you at the airport.

A gift opens doors for the one who gives it and brings him into the presence of great people.

Proverbs 18:16 GOD'S WORD

ONE WITH GOD

Being united with God is my highest good.
PSALM 73:28 GOD'S WORD

Oil and vinegar don't mix. When you pour one into the other, the two separate, with the oil on top. It's the reason you have to shake your salad dressing every time you use it—to combine these two unlike ingredients.

In the Bible, oil is a symbol of anointing, healing, and prosperity. When you allow God's presence to permeate your life, he brings those same attributes, and they spill over into all areas of your life. God's presence is like the oil in your dressing that covers any bitterness in your life. God's presence makes you one with him as he heals and soothes.

Heavenly God, my greatest desire is to be in your presence, every day. Draw me in by your spirit.
AMEN.

You have loved what is right and hated what is wrong. That is why God, your God, anointed you, rather than your companions, with the oil of joy

Hebrews 1:9 GOD'S WORD

CLEAN HANDS AND FEET

Worship the Lord in the beauty of holiness!
PSALM 96:9 NKJV

A long soak in the tub feels good after a hard day's work. It's difficult to work hard and not get dirty. And even though it feels good to work hard,  clean feels good and smells good, too.

Keeping your spiritual life clean is like a sweet smell and a pretty picture to God. He knows that this world has much to offer that isn't in your best interests. God sees your life as an offering to him, because he knows that staying clean requires extra work. It isn't easy staying holy in this world. But rest assured that it is worth it.

Almighty God, show me any areas of my life that are getting dirty, and then show me how to keep them clean for you.
AMEN.

I am pure, without transgression; I am innocent, and there is no iniquity in me.

Job 33:9 NKJV

GOD IN YOU

*That He may establish your hearts without blame in
holiness before our God and Father.*
1 THESSALONIANS 3:13 NASB

Remember when you learned to ride a two-
wheeled bicycle? Gravity felt like the enemy as it tried

to make you fall and skin your
knees. Then as you practiced
more, you became confident,
your legs got strong, and you
were able to ride longer dis-
tances without falling.

Living in God's presence is
a lot like learning to ride a bike.
You have to learn to balance
yourself in a world that wants you to go in a different
direction. But just like riding a bike, as you spend
more time with God, it begins to feel like second
nature. Living in God's presence becomes as easy as,
well, riding a bike.

*The Bible is like a helmet to us, and God's presence is the
padding we need for protection. Put them on every day.*

You will rest safe and secure, filled with hope and emptied of worry.

Job 11:18 CEV

JOY IN PRAYER

When he prays to God, he will be accepted.
And God will receive him with joy
and restore him to good standing.

JOB 33:26 NLT

Prayer is a multifaceted form of communication with God that includes praise, thanksgiving, and worship. You praise God for all he has done, give

thanks for all he will do, and worship him for who he is. In return, you receive peace, comfort, and the assurance of a loving God who cares about you.

God knows how busy you are, and so when you take time to pray, he is well pleased. There is no set formula for prayer, because God desires you to come to him with joy, not with an agenda. Come to him often with a joyful heart, and be amazed at what God has to say to you.

God, thank you that you want to hear from me,
and that when we talk, you take joy in
the restoration of our relationship.
AMEN.

*Absolutely everything, ranging from
small to large, as you make it a part of
your believing prayer, gets included as
you lay hold of God.*

Matthew 21:22 MSG

MAN'S BEST FRIEND

Your new name will be "Justice and Faithfulness."
ISAIAH 1:26 CEV

Often you will hear dogs described as man's best friend because of their loyalty. They stick to you no matter what the situation and no matter what your mood.

God is our best example of true loyalty. He is the one who has been there since before the beginning of time, who stands closer than a brother, who never leaves you or forsakes you, who loves you when you are unlovable. Faith in God's friendship with you will carry you through the darkest storm, the toughest struggle. And always there is the promise of an ending better than the beginning. Choose God.

Heavenly God, thank you for being my best friend.
Thank you for being faithful when I am not,
and bringing me back to yourself.
AMEN.

Some friends don't help, but a true
friend is closer than your own family.

Proverbs 18:24 CEV

HE DESERVES NOTHING LESS

My mouth will tell about your righteousness,
about your salvation all day long.
PSALM 71:15 GOD'S WORD

Standing at the base of Hoover Dam, looking up at the brick-and-concrete edifice before you, makes  you hope the builder knew what he was doing and put his best work and materials into the project. This structure stands as a monument to his skill and ingenuity.

As you seek God and his part in your life, decide to give him your very best. Determine to make changes in your life that reflect his presence. Praise him with everything you do. Let your lifestyle of worship flow over into every area of your life as a testimony to what God is able to do.

Just as a flaw in the Hoover Dam could cause the
entire structure to fail, avoid anything that
may cause your faith to crumble.

Be on guard. Stand true to what you
believe. Be courageous. Be strong.

1 Corinthians 16:13 NLT

NO MATTER HOW IT LOOKS

"I know the plans I have for you," declares the Lord,
"plans to prosper you and not to harm you,
plans to give you hope and a future."
JEREMIAH 29:11 NIV

When a contractor builds a house, the individual parts can look confusing, but he has blueprints to follow. The blueprints don't tell him how to build the house, just where to put the doors, windows, and walls until the parts become a house.

God gives you the Bible to show how the finished product, your life, should look. You take each part, such as prayer, study, and good morals, and arrange it into the overall blueprint. At first it might look confusing, but as the parts come together, your life begins to look more like the good plan God has for you.

God, when life gets confusing and I don't know
where to turn, remind me that in you
there's always a hope and a future.
AMEN.

He is the Rock; his work is perfect. Everything he
does is just and fair. He is a faithful God who
does no wrong; how just and upright he is!

Deuteronomy 32:4 NLT

GENERATIONAL BLESSINGS

He will receive blessing from the Lord and righteous-
ness from the God of his salvation. Such is the
generation of those who seek him, who seek
the face of the God of Jacob.
PSALM 24:5–6 ESV

Some of your best memories are probably gather-
ings where multiple generations came together to cel-

ebrate and share. It is exciting
to experience the beginning of a
new life, whether it is a wedding, a graduation, or the birth
of a child. Memories are sweet,
and relationships are formed
during these times.

God's family extends beyond this life and
through many generations, becoming a blessing for
past, present, and future generations. His family goes
back to the beginning of time and will never end.
Loving God will cause your influence to extend
beyond today and flow over into other lives. Seek
ways to be a blessing to many.

Heavenly God, thank you for drawing me into your
family and for blessing me as I seek you.
AMEN.

Long, long ago he decided to adopt us into his family through Jesus Christ. What pleasure he took in planning this!

Ephesians 1:5 MSG

SEEKING RELATIONSHIP WITH GOD

God has brought us back to life together with Christ Jesus and has given us a position in heaven with him.

Ephesians 2:6 GOD'S WORD

DEEP DOWN

*You know with all your heart and soul that not
one of all the good promises the LORD
your God gave you has failed.*
JOSHUA 23:14 NIV

In a court of law, witnesses are asked to swear
that they will tell the truth, the whole truth, and noth-

ing but the truth. The law rec-
ognizes that anything less than
the complete truth is a lie and
will not result in the truth of
the matter being known.

God has promised you
that he will fulfill his word to
you. Even if it looks like God
has forgotten you or if it seems your prayer isn't being
answered, know this—God keeps his word. Never
once has he failed to do so, and he never will. Allow
God to replace any doubts you have with remembrance of his goodness.

*Almighty God, I know deep in my heart that you always
keep your promises. Remind me of that often,
especially when I falter.*
AMEN.

*The Lord is faithful to all his promises
and loving toward all he has made.*

Psalm 145:13 NIV

YEARS AND YEARS

Love the Lord your God, obey him, and be loyal
to him. This will be your way of life, and
it will mean a long life for you.
DEUTERONOMY 30:20 GOD'S WORD

They sat on the swing on their front porch, just as they did most evenings. Silver shone in their hair, and laugh lines marked their faces. Still, as he looked over at her, she was as beautiful to him as she was the day they married, so long ago. He couldn't imagine life without her. The longer he was married to her, the more he loved her.

God's presence in your life is like a long happy marriage. You cannot imagine life without him. You look forward to spending time with him, and the more time you spend, the more you want. God's presence makes life worth living.

Lord, you are the love of my life. You are what I live for.
Remind me of your presence more and more.
AMEN.

*Your love means more than life
to me, and I praise you.*

Psalm 63:3 CEV

PEOPLE OF GOD

I will accept you as my people, and I will
be your God. Then you will know that
I was the one who rescued you.
EXODUS 6:7 CEV

Everywhere you look, you see names. On clothing, on billboards, on vehicles, names advertise attrib-

utes and qualities that are
deemed important or desirable,
and that will convince you to buy
a certain product or buy into a
concept.

God says that he has given
you a new name—his name.
When you choose him, you are
saying that you have selected him
above all else. God has done the
same thing—he has chosen you above all others. You
are important to him and you are safe in him. Allow
him to envelop you with his peace and security.
Knowing whose you are brings a sense of peace and
security.

If you were advertising God and had his name on your
shirt, would other people want to buy into him?

*May the God who gives endurance and
encouragement give you a spirit of unity
among yourselves as you follow Christ Jesus.*

Romans 15:5 NIV

AN ETERNAL HOME

*One thing I have asked from the LORD, that I
shall seek: that I may dwell in the house
of the LORD all the days of my life.*
PSALM 27:4 NASB

When you look at nature, housing comes in
many forms. Nests, burrows, caves, webs—all serve

their purpose according to the
creatures that inhabit them and
the young they raise. People live
in different kinds of housing,
too: apartments, houses, even
cars or boxes under a bridge.

The one thing all these
houses have in common is that they are temporary.
God's house is eternal. As God dwells in you, you
become a long-lasting reminder of God's love for this
world and his desire for a personal relationship with
his creation. As you allow God to inhabit every area of
your life, others will see God in you.

*God, thank you for choosing me and for choosing to
make your presence known in my life. Remind
me that others are watching me.*
AMEN.

I heard a voice thunder from the
Throne: "Look! Look! God has moved
into the neighborhood, making his
home with men and women! They're
his people, he's their God.

Revelation 21:3 MSG

LET'S TALK

My heart has heard you say, "Come and talk with me."
And my heart responds, "LORD, I am coming."
PSALM 27:8 NLT

A call from the doctor. A special request to see your boss. A note from the teacher about your child.

Often, not good news. Sometimes, more work. Sometimes, just one more thing to add to your already busy schedule.

You need never worry when God asks you to spend time with him. He always has something new and good for you. He is thrilled when you come willingly and hopefully. Listen for his call, and answer that you want to hear from him. Respond joyfully that you want to spend time with him. He loves to spend time with you.

God, time with you is never wasted. I know that when
I'm busy, I need to spend time with you.
AMEN.

May my prayer come to you at an acceptable time, O Lord. O God, out of the greatness of your mercy, answer me with the truth of your salvation.

Psalm 69:13 GOD'S WORD

LIVING AND LISTENING

*Diligently heed the voice of the Lord your God
and do what is right in His sight.*
EXODUS 15:26 NKJV

Native Americans hunted the buffalo on the Great Plains. When the herd moved, the ground rumbled under their hooves. The natives would press

their ear to the ground and hear the vibrations across hundreds of miles; they could tell several days in advance when a herd was moving their way. Listening was important because their survival depended on it.

Today your life doesn't depend on your hunting abilities, but your survival still depends on careful listening. Knowing God demands your time and energy and hearing God's voice amid all the other voices calling to you requires diligence. Learn to distinguish his voice from others by listening to him carefully.

*Take some time to listen to God's voice. Turn off
the other sounds around you and simply
live and listen—just you and God.*

He who belongs to God
hears what God says.

John 8:47 NIV

PROMISES TO LAST

I will be your God throughout your lifetime—
until your hair is white with age. I made
you, and I will care for you.

ISAIAH 46:4 NLT

Have you considered the implication of a wedding ring? It has no beginning and it has no end. It is

one piece, indivisible. No wonder a ring is used as a symbol of unity.

God's promises are like a ring. They were always there, as was God. They will never end, as God will never end. And the best part is, God's promises are for you—for yesterday, for today, and for tomorrow. You don't have to wait for some special day down the road—you can partake of them now, and forever. He made you, he has counted the hairs on your head, and he cares for you.

Almighty God, thank you that though I am temporal,
you are eternal, and though I am unlovable,
you love me. Thank you for your faithfulness.
AMEN.

God is the real thing—the living God, the eternal King.

Jeremiah 10:10 MSG

THE ULTIMATE SECURITY
SYSTEM

*A person is a fool to store up earthly wealth but
not have a rich relationship with God.*

LUKE 12:21 NLT

Everywhere you turn there are locks. Locks on your home, your car, your bicycle at the bike rack at the library. Locks on your suitcase, your computer case, your briefcase. You put locks on things that are important to you. But your most valuable possession isn't a thing.

In fact, your most valuable possession is your relationship with God. Nothing can steal that from you. It doesn't need to be locked up, but it does need to be protected. You can do that by making sure nothing distracts you from time spent with God. Spend time with him—his presence is safe.

*A home security system requires money to keep it active.
Your spiritual security system requires payment—time
with God—to keep it alive and well.*

The Lord gives perfect peace to those whose faith is firm.

Isaiah 26:3 CEV

LOOK INTO HIS FACE

*Tears of joy will stream down their faces, and I will
lead them home with great care.*
JEREMIAH 31:9 NLT

The woman stared, unable to tear her eyes away,
at the statue of Jesus in his mother's arms. Oblivious
to the passing crowd, she simply
stood and cried. And smiled.

Yes, she smiled. She felt the
pain and sorrow that had passed
between them. She knew, though,
that the pain and sorrow had led
to great victory for both Jesus and
his mother. Victory over death
when he rose from the grave. That
victory is there for you. Look into the face of God, and
let him wash away your pain and fear as you enter his
presence once again. Come into his presence, and be
renewed.

*Thank you, God, for giving me victory through the resur-
rection of your son. Wash away my pain with tears of joy.*
AMEN.

He will renew your life and
sustain you in your old age.

Ruth 4:15 NIV

SEEK THE LORD

*Seek the Lord, all you humble of the land, who do his
just commands; seek righteousness; seek humility.*
ZEPHANIAH 2:3 ESV

Traffic signs are everywhere. Stop, Yield, No
U-Turns, Slower Traffic Keep Right. These signs are

there for your safety and the
safety of everyone else on the
road. Traffic engineers have
your best interests at heart.

God gives you signs to follow too, in the form of lives and
patterns of success in the Bible.
When you do what he says to
do, and when you do what he

does, you'll be doing his will. The best part about
doing God's will is that it's what is best for you. God
always has your best interests at heart.

*Righteous God, my heart knows you want what is best
for me. Help me to communicate that to my mind.*
AMEN.

I do nothing on my own authority, but speak just as the Father taught me.

John 8:28 ESV

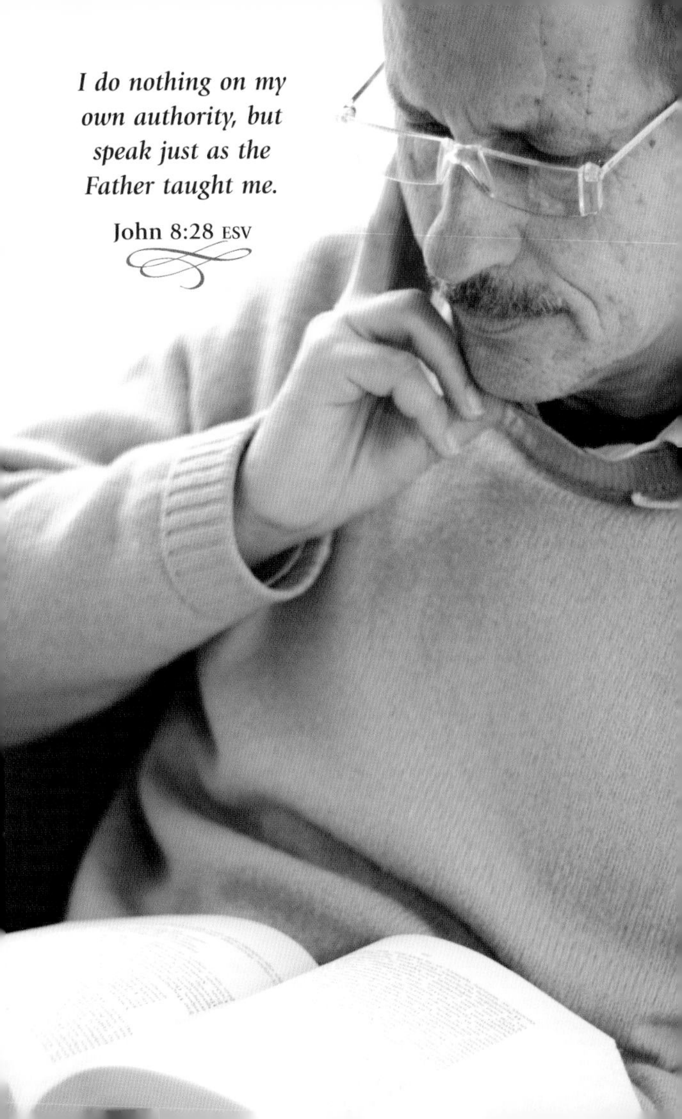

GUIDING LIGHT

*I am yours. Save me, because I have
searched for your guiding principles.*
PSALM 119:94 GOD'S WORD

A lighthouse warns ships of various dangers,
including shoals, submerged sandbars, or a shallow
beach. If the ship's captain
believes he knows better than
the lighthouse, he could be in
danger.

The Bible is God's light-
house in your life. Through it,
God shows you the best way and
warns you of danger. If you fol-
low him, your path is made clear and safe. Ignore
him, and you could run aground. Follow him by
studying the Bible for his direction and allowing him
to be your light. How comforting to know you don't
have to find your own way and that he leads you in his
paths.

*Lighthouses have become symbols of safety in a
dangerous world. Look for ways to be a
lighthouse in your own neighborhood.*

Even though I walk through the valley of the shadow of death, I fear no evil, for You are with me.

Psalm 23:4 NASB

LAW-ABIDING CITIZEN

He commanded Judah to seek the LORD, the God of their fathers, and to obey his laws and commands.
2 CHRONICLES 14:4 NIV

The puppy had learned his lessons in obedience school well. He sat, lay down, stayed, and came on cue. One day he got separated from his owner while they walked in the park. When at last he saw her, he

ran toward her, oblivious of all else. His owner saw the approaching bicyclist and commanded her dog, "Down!" Instantly he dropped to the ground, and the cyclist went past.

The puppy obeyed because he'd been taught to. There is safety in obeying the one who knows what's best for you. God always knows what is best, because he knows everything. Obedience is not negative or restricting. Obedience demonstrates that you love and trust God.

Sometimes God will require you to do something you don't understand. Don't worry—obedience will bring understanding. Trust him to bring you that understanding.

Trust God from the bottom of your heart; don't try to figure out everything on your own. Listen for God's voice in everything you do, everywhere you go; he's the one who will keep you on track

Proverbs 3:5–6 MSG

TESTING, TESTING 1-2-3

You shall remember all the way which the Lord your God has led you in the wilderness these forty years, that He might humble you, testing you, to know what was in your heart, whether you would keep His commandments or not.

DEUTERONOMY 8:2 NASB

Cars are tested to make sure they're safe. Even food needs to be tested to ensure quality and freshness. Everywhere you see the evidence of how testing

has made a product better, safer, and more useful.

While most testing is to prove an item's worth to you, God tests you to confirm what he already knows about you. He never takes you into a situation unless he knows that you have already demonstrated the ability to succeed. He tests you for your benefit, to give you victory, to give you confidence for the next hurdle. God already knows that with him, you are a winner.

When David faced Goliath, he remembered his past victories over the lion and the bear. Ask God to remind you of your past victories when you feel you are facing an obstacle or situation.

You are a shield around me, O Lord; you bestow glory on me and lift up my head.

Psalm 3:3 NIV

FOLLOW THE LEADER

See, the Lord your God has set the land before you. Go up, take possession, as the Lord, the God of your fathers, has told you. Do not fear or be dismayed.
DEUTERONOMY 1:21 ESV

In the corporate world, leadership skills are crucial to advancement. Being able to work independently of direct supervision is a skill much sought after.

The best leaders start out as exceptional followers.

God has a plan that goes one step further than corporate strategy. He doesn't stop with just training leaders. He trains leaders to train leaders. He has given you his instruction manual—the Bible. And he's given you a long-term on-the-job training deal—your life. As you take on this assignment, remember that with God, you cannot fail. Study the manual, and put his policies and procedures into everyday practice.

God, thank you for seeing the finished works of your hands in me. Teach me your ways so that I can teach others to do the same.
AMEN.

I will teach them—this time I will teach them my power and might. Then they will know that my name is the LORD.

Jeremiah 16:21 NIV

LIVING IN
GOD'S LOVE

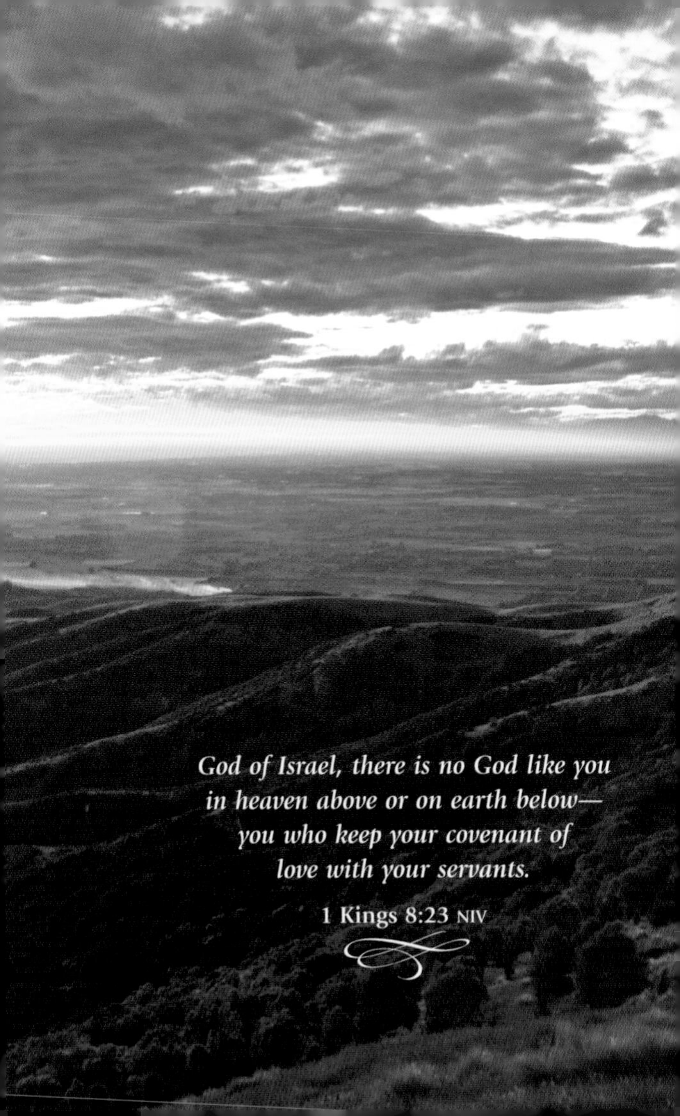

*God of Israel, there is no God like you
in heaven above or on earth below—
you who keep your covenant of
love with your servants.*

1 Kings 8:23 NIV

BEYOND IMAGINATION

Because of his great love for us, God, who is rich in
mercy, made us alive with Christ.
EPHESIANS 2:4–5 NIV

When you think of the word *rich,* you might imagine money, expensive cars, or big houses. Maybe a cruise is your idea of being rich, or maybe it's having  someone clean house for you. Whether you're currently wealthy or hoping to be on your way there, there's always room for more.

When you put *God* and *rich* in the same sentence, however, the images probably change. God has much more than money and cars to offer those who seek him. He offers you a relationship with him richer than you could ever imagine. He offers love, peace, and eternal life. He offers you blessings beyond imagination.

God of all creation, remind me that my wealth
isn't in things, that my real wealth is in you.
Thank you for all you give.
AMEN.

Remember the LORD your God, for it is he who gives you power to get wealth, that he may confirm his covenant that he swore to your fathers, as it is this day.

Deuteronomy 8:18 ESV

FAITH FOR TODAY

Having been justified by faith, we have peace with
God through our Lord Jesus Christ.
ROMANS 5:1 NASB

When you turn on a light switch, you have faith that the light will come on. You don't necessarily understand how it works, and you probably don't  care about the generators, transformers, and conductors that got the electricity to the switch. All you care is that the light comes on.

Just as you don't understand everything about electricity, you don't always understand about God and his plan for your life. God knows that. All he asks is that you believe what he says. When you believe him, you can come to him whenever you want. He's never too busy to hear from you. Come into God's presence today. He's ready whenever you are.

Resistance causes electricity to lose power as it travels
from the generator to the light switch. Don't
diminish God's power in your life by resisting
him—welcome his presence in your life.

*Your faith should not be
in the wisdom of men but
in the power of God.*

1 Corinthians 2:5 NKJV

FAITHFUL ONE

You shall teach them diligently to your children,
and shall talk of them when you sit in your house,
when you walk by the way, when you lie down,
and when you rise up.
DEUTERONOMY 6:7 NKJV

Finishing a task requires faithfulness. There will always be other things you'd rather be doing.

Faithfulness requires you to stick to it until the work is complete, no matter how messy or unpleasant it may get.

God is a faithful God. He does what he says he will do. And one of the things he says he will do is finish the work he started in you. You are a work in progress. Don't get discouraged when it feels like the work will never be done. Take heart in knowing that God always does good work. And he always finishes what he starts.

God, thank you that you see the finished project in
me and that you believe I am worth the
effort. Give me more faith, God.
AMEN.

I'm convinced that God, who began this good work in you, will carry it through to completion on the day of Christ Jesus.

Philippians 1:6 GOD'S WORD

MORE THAN SKIN DEEP

Give unto the LORD the glory due to His name;
worship the LORD in the beauty of holiness.
PSALM 29:2 NKJV

Every culture has its definition of what constitutes beauty. Some cultures encourage svelte physiques; some prefer voluptuous curves. Some cultures idolize light skin and blue or green eyes, while others prefer dark skin tones and eyes. Even within these cultures the ideal can change over time, according to fad and fashion.

How comforting to know that God's definition of beauty remains a constant. You are beautiful in God's eyes as you seek him and come into his presence. God loves to see you living a holy life, choosing to please him, desiring to praise and worship him. He looks past the skin and into your spirit, and he is well-pleased.

While your concept of beauty may change with time or
trend, God sees you as he created you—perfect and
complete in him. His idea of beauty doesn't change.

*What matters is not your outer appearance—
the styling of your hair, the jewelry you wear,
the cut of your clothes—but your inner
disposition. Cultivate inner beauty, the
gentle, gracious kind that God delights in.*

1 Peter 3:3–4 MSG

FREED FROM CAPTIVITY

I will set them free from slavery and let them live
safely in their own land. Then they will
know that I am the Lord.
EZEKIEL 34:27 CEV

Being held captive doesn't require you to be imprisoned. You can be held captive by fears, by pho-

bias, or even by relationships. You were created to have free will, to have the opportunity to make your own choices about your destiny. You were not created to be held hostage.

God made you that way, because if he forced you to love him, that wouldn't be love. If he forced you to choose him, that wouldn't be choice. When you love God and freely choose to follow him, your life can be an example to others of the truest meaning of love. Choose God—and choose true freedom.

God, thank you for trusting me enough to free me and to
set me as an example to show others how to be free in you.
AMEN.

Christ has set us free! This means we are really free. Now hold on to your freedom and don't ever become slaves of the Law again.

Galatians 5:1 CEV

CAREGIVER

God All-Powerful, please do something! Look down
from heaven and see what's happening to this vine.
PSALM 80:14 CEV

Grapes grow on vines that have to be trained to
wrap around a trellis. Left to their own devices, the
vines would climb anything, including each other,

and eventually choke each other.
The vine grower takes time and
care pruning the vines, cultivating
stronger growth and maximum
yield of fruit.

Just as the vine grower trains
his vines to grow in a certain
direction, God trains you to grow
into his presence. He prunes those areas of your life
that are unfruitful or harmful. God's goal is to produce strong spiritual growth for you that is reflected
in the spiritual fruit that others see. Allow God to do
his work in you. He cares how you turn out.

All-knowing God, you have a plan for me,
and that plan is good. Cultivate in me
a spirit of growth and maturity for you.
AMEN.

The seed shall be prosperous, the vine shall give its fruit, the ground shall give her increase, and the heavens shall give their dew—I will cause the remnant of this people to possess all these.

Zechariah 8:12 NKJV

AND THE WINNER IS . . .

Our God is the God of victories. The Almighty
LORD is our escape from death.
PSALM 68:20 GOD'S WORD

An Olympic race pits the best in the world against each other, each vying for the gold medal. Fractions of seconds separate the victor from the close finishers. Each racer seeks the victory.

God's victories are in people; his rewards in lives changed. He doesn't seek medals or trophies; he seeks those who claim him as their God, as lord of their life. God wins when you win. And so God sets you up to win. He never takes you into a situation unless he already knows the outcome. Stick with God—make him first in your life, and he will make you a winner.

Focus your efforts on those things that are eternal—
God and his plan for you. God treasures
you now and forever more.

*This is the only race worth running.
I've run hard right to the finish,
believed all the way.*

2 Timothy 4:7 MSG

PRAISE GOD

*Sing to the LORD! Give praise to the LORD! He rescues
the life of the needy from the hands of the wicked.*
JEREMIAH 20:13 NIV

Wolves howl, frogs croak, and birds sing. Almost
everywhere you look, you can see evidence of creation

making a joyful noise, often for
no apparent reason. Perhaps
they are simply singing the
praises of their Creator.

If God would give voices to
his lesser creation, how much
more so to the ones created in his

own image? You were made to sing the praises of
your God. Praise lifts your heart, changes your focus,
and pleases God immensely. Praise also brings you
from discouragement to victory. Praise God often.
Tell the enemy that you are not defeated. And thank
God for your victory.

*Victorious God, you are commander-in-chief of all my
battles, and I am a winner because of you.*
AMEN.

A thief is only there to steal and kill and destroy. I came so they can have real and eternal life, more and better life than they ever dreamed of.

John 10:10 MSG

TOGETHER WITH GOD

*Though I walk in the midst of trouble, You will
revive me; You will stretch forth Your hand
against the wrath of my enemies.*
PSALM 138:7 NASB

A man was caught in an avalanche. After two
days, he was found alive, buried under five feet of
snow. When asked what had
kept him alive, he said he
strongly felt the presence of
God. He couldn't explain it further than that.

When you feel as if you are
buried under a mountain of
snow—or paperwork or laundry—know that God is
nearby. God knows you can't get out by yourself. He
works through your weakness, making you strong.
God is on the other side of that mountain, and he is
making a way through for you.

*If you feel as if you're always swamped, prayerfully ask
God to show you what changes you need to make.
There is no mountain bigger than God.*

God has done all this, so that we will look for him and reach out and find him. He isn't far from any of us.

Acts 17:27 CEV

MORE THAN A PASSING GRADE

As for God, His way is blameless; the word of the Lord is tested; He is a shield to all who take refuge in Him.
2 SAMUEL 22:31 NASB

Car manufacturers are stringent about safety testing their vehicles. A five-star crash rating is the best a vehicle can get, and it is included in commercials about the car. Car manufacturers want you to believe their vehicles are the best and safest on the road.

God knows that his plan for you is the best and safest plan. Through Jesus, God has already gone through everything he asks you to do. Jesus experienced betrayal and punishment for things he didn't do. God never asks you to do anything he hasn't already done, and he promises you the best rating of all—far beyond five stars.

God, when I get my eyes off you and onto the problem, remind me you are already there, ahead of me, leading the way.
AMEN.

Well done, my good and faithful servant. You have been faithful in handling this small amount, so now I will give you many more responsibilities. Let's celebrate together!

Matthew 25:23 NLT

MISSION: POSSIBLE

With God everything is possible.
MATTHEW 19:26 NLT

There are days when it seems that everything is a struggle. Right from the moment you set your feet on the floor, nothing goes right. On those days, you prob-

ably wonder why you even bothered to get out of bed that morning.

But then there are days when you feel God's presence strongly, and you know he is right there with you. Like a well-tuned orchestra, your world sounds right. You are invincible. In God's presence, you can do anything. And even when things don't feel so great, remember that God is still there, waiting for you to reach out to him.

Before you put your feet on the floor in the morning, ask God what his plan is for the day. Include him in all you do.

If any of you need wisdom, you should ask God, and it will be given to you. God is generous and won't correct you for asking.

James 1:5 CEV

LIVING IN
GOD'S BLESSING

I do all things for the sake of the gospel, so that I may become a fellow partaker of it.

1 Corinthians 9:23 NASB

CLEAN AND HOLY LIVES

*Live in peace with everyone, and seek
to live a clean and holy life.*
HEBREWS 12:14 NLT

Every time you turn on the television, someone is advertising a new and improved body soap, a better toilet bowl cleaner, or a "tough on stains but gentle-on your clothes" stain remover. Everywhere you look, people are concerned about physical cleanliness.

Living in God's presence requires spiritual cleanliness, too. His presence is cleansing. When you pray you release your cares to him. When you read the Bible you create an atmosphere of calm and peace. God asks you to live in his peace every moment of every day. Relax, enjoy his company, and get refreshed and renewed.

*God, cleanse me, renew me, and refresh
me so I can show you and your holiness.*
AMEN.

Jesus said, "If I don't wash you, you can't be part of what I'm doing."

John 13:8 MSG

KEEPING IN TOUCH

He does what's best for those who fear him—
hears them call out, and saves them.
PSALM 145:19 MSG

Before cellular phones were popular, if you wanted to call someone while you were away from home, you had to find a pay phone. It probably wasn't something you did on a regular basis, especially if you just wanted to call a friend and chat.

What a blessing to serve a God who doesn't require special equipment, like a telephone, to be able to talk with him. Wherever you are, whatever you're doing, you can stop and talk to God. Don't wait until there is an emergency. Take a moment now, and talk with God. Just like an old friend, he has lots of good things to share with you.

Today, find some extra time to spend in prayer with God.
Pray at the traffic light, in the elevator, at the market.

*Heed the sound of my cry for help, my
King and my God, for to You I pray.*

Psalm 5:2 NASB

GOD IS JOY

Let all who seek You rejoice and be glad in You.
PSALM 70:4 NASB

Christopher Columbus set sail from Europe, convinced he would find a new world on the other side of the ocean. At the time, most people were sure the world was flat, and they believed Columbus would sail off the other edge. No doubt Columbus found great joy in proving them wrong.

When you begin to wonder if God's promises are true for you, when your friends question your walk of faith, or when it seems as if God is far from you, remember this—God is true, he knows your doubts, and he's as close as your next breath. Draw near to God, and feel the warmth of his presence.

God, as you draw me into your presence, I leave
behind the worries and cares of this day.
Thank you for your peace.
AMEN.

The Lord is good, a refuge in times of trouble.
He cares for those who trust in him.

Nahum 1:7 NIV

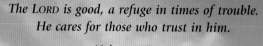

SOUND ADVICE

There are many plans in a man's heart, nevertheless the Lord's counsel—that will stand.
PROVERBS 19:21 NKJV

If you have a problem with your car, you go to a mechanic. If your mechanic said you needed something fixed, you would listen. If your mechanic told you to follow certain steps to maintain your car, you would probably follow the instructions.

When you're seeking direction for your life, go to the one who knows what's best for you. God has a plan for your life, how best to use your particular personality, experiences, and passions. He knows exactly how you fit into his plan, and his desire is to show you what your part is. Listen to God's advice, and follow his instructions.

While God's plan may not always be what you had in mind, know that his will is always best for you.

True wisdom and power are with God;
counsel and understanding are his.

Job 12:13 NLT

NEVER FAR AWAY

Seek God while he's here to be found, pray to him while he's close at hand.
ISAIAH 55:6 MSG

Echoes are created when sounds bounce off solid surfaces and reflect back to you. You don't hear an

echo in a small room, because the sound bounces back so quickly your brain thinks it is part of the original sound. When you are in a large empty room, however, the sound takes longer to return to you, and you hear an echo.

Unlike echoes, your prayers go directly to God. There is no delay because of distance or interference. God hears every prayer and answers each one at the best possible time for you. Prayer brings you closer to God and deepens your relationship with him.

God, I want to have more of you in my life. Open the windows of heaven to me through our prayer time.
AMEN.

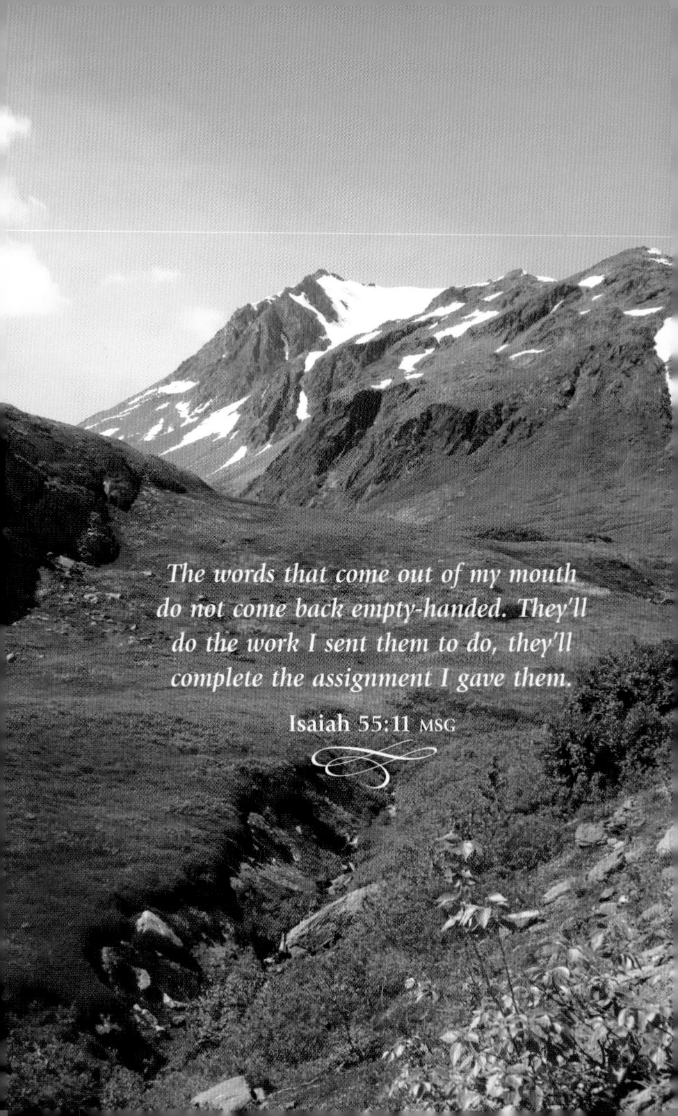

*The words that come out of my mouth
do not come back empty-handed. They'll
do the work I sent them to do, they'll
complete the assignment I gave them.*

Isaiah 55:11 MSG

INTIMACY WITH GOD

Jacob called the name of the place Peniel: "For I have seen God face to face, and my life is preserved."
GENESIS 32:30 NKJV

When you look into the face of a child, you often see a reflection of the parents. The eyes, the nose, the

smile, all testify to their lineage. Often, as people age, they become more like one parent than the other, not just in looks, but also in mannerism and attitude.

Spending time with God and living according to his will and plan for your life will cause you to take on his character and his attitude. Just as your parents took joy in seeing you grow up to be like them, God takes much joy as you change into his likeness and image.

God, more than anything else I want to look and act just like you. Remove anything in me that isn't from you.
AMEN.

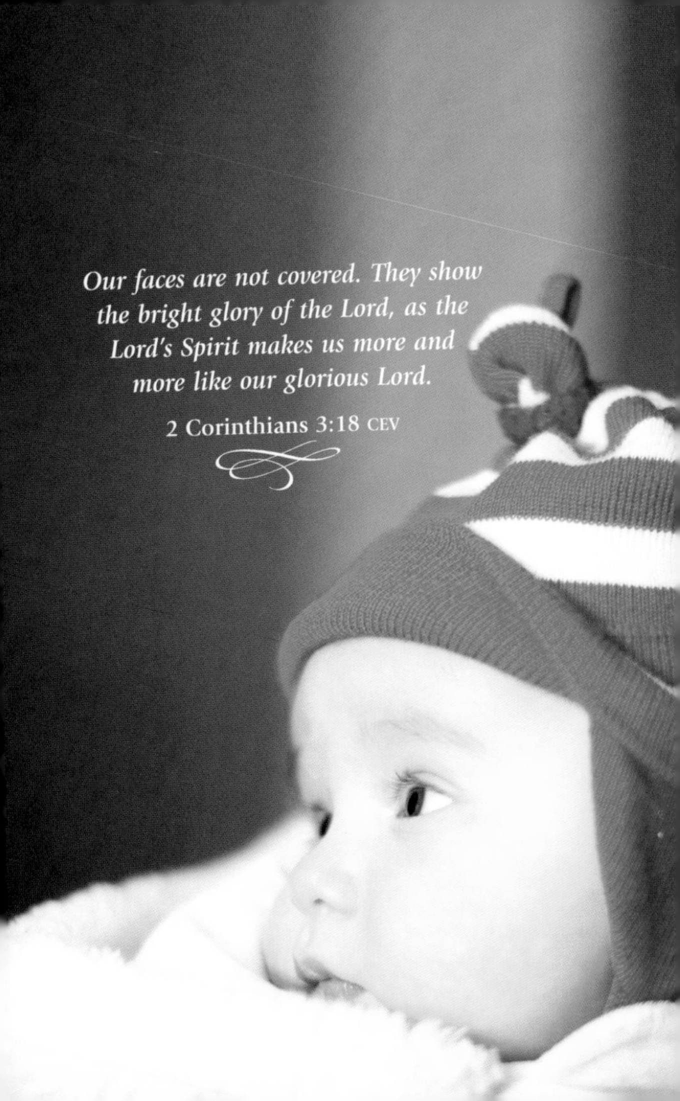

Our faces are not covered. They show the bright glory of the Lord, as the Lord's Spirit makes us more and more like our glorious Lord.

2 Corinthians 3:18 CEV

MORE TIME TOGETHER

My soul thirsts for God, for the living God.
When can I go and meet with God?
PSALM 42:2 NIV

When the rain stops falling for a prolonged period, the soil dries up and blows away, creating a  desert. When it does rain, there's nothing to absorb the water, and the water simply runs off. To change a desert into productive ground, you bring in lots of top-soil and plants to hold the water.

When your walk of faith feels like a desert, when your prayer life lacks power, and when your meditation and quiet time lose their foundation, remember this—this desert doesn't have to be permanent. As you move forward into the bounty of God's presence, prepare to blossom as you meet once again with God.

Even the desert blooms when given enough rain. In your desert times, seek ways to show God's glory in your life.

Be alert, be present. I'm about to do something brand-new. It's bursting out! Don't you see it? There it is! I'm making a road through the desert, rivers in the badlands.

Isaiah 43:19 MSG

A CLEAR VANTAGE POINT

*Many people shall come and say, "Come, and let us go
up to the mountain of the Lord, to the house of the
God of Jacob; He will teach us His ways,
and we shall walk in His paths."*

ISAIAH 2:3 NKJV

Sailing ships from the 1800s had a small platform
on the main mast called a "crow's nest." A sailor
climbed the mast when
fog, high seas, or thick
ice obstructed the cap-
tain's view. The captain
was then able to make
decisions to steer the
ship to safety.

God is like the
sailor in the crow's nest—he has a better view of
what's ahead than you do. Allow him to direct your
paths. As you set aside time for God, consider what
you will do with that time. As he teaches you his ways,
decide how to demonstrate his teachings into your
life.

*Almighty God, show me your ways and show me how I
can incorporate them into my life. My desire
is to walk with you always.*
AMEN.

*I will cause my people and their homes
around my holy hill to be a blessing. And I
will send showers, showers of blessings,
which will come just when they are needed.*

Ezekiel 34:26 NLT

WHICH ONE IS WHICH?

*You are to distinguish between what
is holy and what is ordinary.*
LEVITICUS 10:10 NLT

When treasury agents train to be able to identify counterfeit money, they study the real thing. They know authentic bills from every angle, from every test imaginable, including light, feel, ink, and weight. By knowing what real money looks like, they're able to spot counterfeit bills.

As you seek more of God's presence in your life, you will be able to distinguish what is from God and what is not. God has created you to be set apart for his service and not to be worn down by the things of life. Cast aside the ordinary in favor of his best for you—extraordinary blessings are yours for the taking.

*Heavenly God, take me beyond the ordinary of this
world and into your extraordinary promises.
You alone are the one my heart desires.*
AMEN.

Good people will keep on doing right,
and God's people will always be holy.

Revelation 22:11 CEV

FREE TO ENTER

Lift your heads, you gates. Be lifted, you ancient
doors, so that the king of glory may come in.
PSALM 24:7 GOD'S WORD

As you choose to live in God's presence, you
make changes to your life and clean up those areas

where you know God is working on you. You study the
Bible, hang out with some new
friends, and maybe even get
some new hobbies. All these
changes are intended to bring
you into God's presence.

Your relationship with
God isn't one-sided, however. While he welcomes the
changes you make in your life, he also reminds you
that he is a part of those changes. Living in God's
presence isn't something you do now and then leave.
Open your life to him today so that he may enter in.

All-knowing God, reveal any area of my life that needs to
be changed, cleansed, or purged. I want you in my life.
AMEN.

*Let us go right into the presence of God,
with true hearts fully trusting him.*

Hebrews 10:22 NLT

NO MORE OBSTACLES

*He renews my strength. He guides me along right
paths, bringing honor to his name.*
PSALM 23:3 NLT

In steeplechase races, horse and rider speed
around a track as they jump tall fences. Going around
the fence brings disqualification. Going through the

fence slows down the horse
and might cause a fall. The
fences are challenging but
jumpable. In the last couple of
furlongs there are no jumps to
clear, and the rider urges the
horse to go as fast as it can to
the end of the race.

Your walk of faith may often feel like a steeplechase. Everywhere you turn, obstacles have to be
overcome, not just avoided. Remember that nothing
is impossible for your God. Together, you and God
are winners.

*God, remind me that with you, I can do anything.
I can overcome all obstacles and finish
this race of life victoriously.*
AMEN.

Such a large crowd of witnesses is all around us! So we must get rid of everything that slows us down, especially the sin that just won't let go. And we must be determined to run the race that is ahead of us.

Hebrews 12:1 CEV

THE KING'S DELIGHT

Righteous lips are the delight of a king, and he loves
him who speaks what is right.
PROVERBS 16:13 ESV

A recent survey showed that the number one fear
of most people is public speaking. There are courses
and clubs that train people to
overcome their fear by using for-
mats and techniques to relieve
tension so that the message comes
across clearly.

What a joy to know that God
doesn't require special training
from you so that you can talk
with him. Spending time with
God opens channels of communi-
cation that go beyond mere words. God knows that
sometimes your thoughts will be jumbled and your
prayers will be incoherent. Pray from the heart, and
please God with your presence, not just your words.

God, you are the one I set my sights on and fashion my
life after. Give me courage to rely on you.
AMEN.

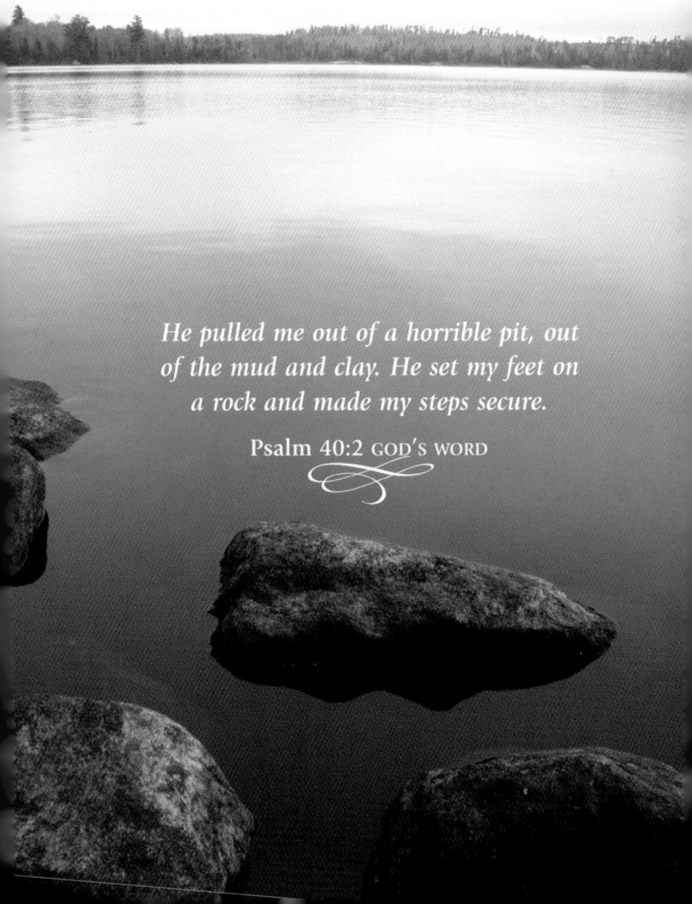

He pulled me out of a horrible pit, out of the mud and clay. He set my feet on a rock and made my steps secure.

Psalm 40:2 GOD'S WORD

A GIFT IN RETURN

Dear friends, God is good. So I beg you to offer your
bodies to him as a living sacrifice, pure and pleasing.
That's the most sensible way to serve God.
ROMANS 12:1 CEV

A child walked more than ten miles to the ocean and back to get a seashell to give her teacher. The teacher marveled that the child would walk so far to bring back just a seashell. The child replied that the journey was part of the gift.

When you consider the awe-someness of God, it's hard to com-prehend a gift worthy of him. After all he's done in your life, what could you give him that he doesn't already have? You give him what he gave you—your life. By living a life that pleases God, by seeking him as first in your life, you're giving him the best you have in return for the best he had.

When you buy a gift for someone you care about, you
choose carefully and thoughtfully. Carefully and thought-
fully choose the way you live as the gift you give to God.

Each of you must bring a gift in proportion to the way the LORD your God has blessed you.

Deuteronomy 16:17 NIV

PROTECTED FROM HARM

My shield is with God, who saves the upright in heart.

PSALM 7:10 ESV

When you hear the word *protection*, there are many images that come to mind: underarm deodorant, life insurance, air bags, seat belts, vaccinations.  All these forms of protection have one thing in common—they come from outside you. You hope that they do the job.

In contrast, God is your protection from the dangers of this world. He has created you in such a way that you crave his presence. His presence isn't just applied to your outside—he becomes a part of your life. As such, you have no fear of being separated from him or his protection. And that's the best hope of all.

God, as I seek your presence, show me how to include you in all I do. I want to spend every moment with you.
AMEN.

May the God of hope fill you with all joy and peace in believing, so that by the power of the Holy Spirit you may abound in hope.

Romans 15:13 ESV

WHEN THE DAWN COMES

*The LORD will bring me out of my darkness into
the light, and I will see his righteousness.*
MICAH 7:9 NLT

In ancient times, some cultures believed that the
ocean swallowed up the sun each evening and that the

sun escaped the following morning.
The modern understanding, of
course, is that the earth rotates
around the sun, and there's never a
time when some part of the earth
isn't lit by the sun.

God has created a world where
there is no complete darkness. He
promises that there are no completely dark times in
him. No matter what it looks like, he is always there,
lighting the way for you.

*Sometimes it's hard to tell the difference between a
sunrise and a sunset unless you know the
direction you're facing. There is promise in both.*

The day and the night are yours. You set
the moon and the sun in their places.

Psalm 74:16 GOD'S WORD

BLACK AND WHITE

Once more you shall see the distinction between the righteous and the wicked, between one who serves God and one who does not serve him.
MALACHI 3:18 ESV

If the keys on a piano were all white or all black, it would be easy to make a mistake, and the music would be discordant. Where there is no distinction

from right and wrong, it is impossible to choose correctly.

God has given you specific guidelines for telling right from wrong. He has given you the Ten Commandments as an example of what is right and what is not. When you choose to live according to God's purpose for your life, you will look different to most people around you. Of course, the most important distinction is that you will be pleasing to God.

God, as I seek you in my life, as I choose between right and wrong, encourage me to look different from other people.
AMEN.

God is working in you, giving you the
desire to obey him and the power
to do what pleases him.

Philippians 2:13 NLT

RAISE YOUR VOICE

I sing to God, the Praise-Lofty,
and find myself safe and saved.
PSALM 18:3 MSG

Wolves bay at the moon, birds sing from the trees, and even the frogs have their own nighttime chorale, croaking their secret rhythm. God has created

a mass choir to sing his praises.

God created you to sing his praises too. You can sing to God with your voice, with your actions, even with your attitude of thankfulness. Praising God can be done anywhere, anytime. Sing to God—he has given you vocal cords for a reason. Shout his praises for all to hear—you can never tell him too much or too often how much you love him.

Sing and shout God's praises more than the praises of
anyone else, including a sports team. God
delights in the praises of his people.

*If they kept quiet, the stones would do it
for them, shouting praise.*

Luke 19:40 MSG

LIVING UNDER
GOD'S DIRECTION

*The report of your obedience has reached
to all; therefore I am rejoicing over you.*

Romans 16:19 NASB

MORE THAN IMAGINED

God was most especially kind to Hannah. She had three more sons and two daughters!
1 Samuel 2:21 MSG

In the Old Testament, Hannah had been unable to have children for many years. She prayed many times for a child, and always her prayer seemed to go unanswered. It wasn't until she promised to give the

child to God that her prayer was answered. She had a son, named Samuel, and when he was three years old, she took him to the temple and left him there to be raised as a priest and prophet in God's service. After that, she had five more children.

When it seems as if your prayers aren't being answered, look at whom the prayer benefits. When you pray to benefit God and his plans, you will often be amazed at how you also are a beneficiary. Be prepared to have your prayers answered. It may change what you pray for.

All-Knowing God, thank you that you haven't always given me what I asked for. Thank you for the prayers you are answering now.
AMEN.

Be joyful in hope, patient in affliction, faithful in prayer.

Romans 12:12 NIV

A MUCH-WANTED GIFT

He answered their prayers, because they trusted in him.
1 CHRONICLES 5:20 NIV

She taught in the public school system for over thirty years, praying with her students every day. Her motto had been, "I'm going to pray in my classroom every day until they tell me to stop." She understood that public prayer could result in her dismissal. But she also knew people needed to hear about God. One of her former students said of her, "She gave me a gift that could have cost her everything. Instead, it gave me everything I need."

Trusting in God brings great blessing to you and to others. Be encouraged when you remember that God hears and answers every prayer.

Prayer is meant to be a two-way communication with you and God. Listen at least as much as you pray.

The prayer of an innocent person is
powerful, and it can help a lot.

James 5:16 CEV

BLESSINGS FROM HEAVEN

God blesses those whose hearts are pure,
for they will see God.
MATTHEW 5:8 NLT

There are few things as beautiful as a fresh fall of snow. The white cover glistens like diamonds, mak-

ing everything look crystal clean. Trees have new coats, and even the mud-splashed streets look clean. Still, the mud is underneath; the snow cannot remove the mud, just cover it.

When you come into God's presence, you bring a little dirt with you from your past experiences. However, as you spend time with him, his blessings don't just cover the dirt, they actually remove it. In God's presence, there is cleansing and renewing. Spend time with God today, and see how good you feel afterward.

Time with God can feel refreshing like a shower on a
hot day, comforting like a familiar friend,
and fulfilling like a job well done.

Surely God is good to Israel, to those who are pure in heart!

Psalm 73:1 NASB

BEYOND NUMBER

I will tell others about your miracles,
which are more than I can count.
PSALM 40:5 GOD'S WORD

~

In an old cartoon, Charlie Brown asks Lucy why people don't like him. She tells him to divide a piece of paper into 100 squares; if they run out of room,

they'll turn the page over. Charlie really wasn't looking for that many reasons.

On the opposite spectrum, consider how good God has been to you. If you took a piece of paper and divided it into 100 squares, you would need many sheets of paper to properly record all he has done for you. What a joy to serve a God who cannot be out given, who never runs short, and always has more than enough.

Immeasurable God, remind me of your goodness
to me again and again. Show me how to tell
others so they will want more of you.
AMEN.

*I will whistle for them to gather them together,
for I have redeemed them; and they will
be as numerous as they were before.*

Zechariah 10:8 NASB

FIRST IMPRESSIONS

Moses hid his face because he was afraid to look at God.
EXODUS 3:6 GOD'S WORD

If you've ever watched a moth flutter around a light bulb, you've probably wondered what the attraction is. If the moth gets too close to the light bulb, it

will die from the heat. Still, there is something innate in moths that drives them to seek the light.

God has created you to seek him. He has designed you to crave him, the way a moth craves the light. Unlike the moth, if you get close to God in an intimate and loving relationship, you won't die. On the contrary, you will live. Regardless of what your relationship with God has been in the past, seek his presence in your life.

Moths die from the heat because they weren't created to be near the light. You were created to be near the source of all life—God.

Don't be afraid, because I am with you.
Don't be intimidated; I am your God.
I will strengthen you. I will help you.
I will support you with my
victorious right hand.

Isaiah 41:10 GOD'S WORD

STRONG SHOULDERS

*The Lord hasn't lost his powerful strength;
he can still hear and answer prayers.*
ISAIAH 59:1 CEV

In Greek mythology, Atlas was punished by having to carry the world on his shoulders forever. He managed to trick Hercules into holding it for him for

a while, but Hercules was smarter and tricked Atlas back into his punishment.

Unlike the Greek gods, your God is a God of love. When it feels like you're carrying the world on your shoulders, call on him. Jesus said his yoke was *easy* and his burden was *light*. When you name your cares and concerns as "easy and light," you diminish their impact on you. Give your cares to God—he is more than able to take them for you.

*Loving God, thank you for caring for me. Show me how
to rest in you and to release my burdens to you.*
AMEN.

Pile your troubles on God's shoulders—he'll carry your load, he'll help you out. He'll never let good people topple into ruin.

Psalm 55:22 MSG

A HELPING HAND

You, O God, do see trouble and grief; you consider it to take it in hand. The victim commits himself to you; you are the helper of the fatherless.
PSALM 10:14 NIV

The young boy stubbornly pushed his mother's hand away as she tried to steady him on his new bicycle. "I can do it myself," he declared. She sighed, waiting for the inevitable. Moments later, he was on the ground—again. Finally, he looked up at her and asked, "Will you help me next time?"

Relying on your own efforts to accomplish your goals diminishes one of God's characteristics—he loves to share with you. God likes it when you come to him for help and acknowledge that he is the only source. Rely on God today for everything you need. There is no shame in admitting you need his help.

God, when I forget, remind me that you love to meet my needs, and that in you, there is never any lack.
AMEN.

Leave your fatherless children, I will preserve them alive; and let your widows trust in Me.

Jeremiah 49:11 NKJV

STRENGTHENING THE FOUNDATION

Night and day we pray most earnestly that we may see
you again and supply what is lacking in your faith.
1 THESSALONIANS 3:10 NIV

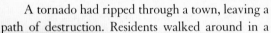

A tornado had ripped through a town, leaving a path of destruction. Residents walked around in a  daze, not knowing where to begin the rebuilding of their town and their lives. So much had been lost, including their belief that nothing like this would happen to them.

Without hope, it is difficult to carry on. Hope is the foundation of your faith. Without it, you cannot expect to weather the storms of life. Your belief that God can make a difference is foundational to your faith. Strengthen your faith today—show others how strong your relationship with God is by praying. When prayers are answered, everyone's faith is strengthened.

Answered prayer should first bolster your faith and
then the faith of others around you. Be prepared
for someone to ask you for prayer today.

We fasted and earnestly prayed that our God would take care of us, and he heard our prayer.

Ezra 8:23 NLT

NO MORE SECRETS!

*If we had forgotten the name of our God or spread out
our hands to a foreign god, would not God have
discovered it, since he knows the secrets of the heart?*
PSALM 44:20–21 NIV

The whisper game starts with a phrase whispered in the ear of the first person, who in turn whispers it to the next person, and so on around the group.

The phrase, spoken aloud by the last person, is usually not even close to the original whisper, demonstrating how different people hear the same thing in different ways.

Unlike the whisper game, God shouts his love and desire for you from the rising of the sun, to singing of the birds, and on through his gift of his son, Jesus. Listen closely to what God is telling you, and then, in turn, sing it loud and clear for others to hear.

*God, when I am not listening carefully, draw me close to
you. I want to always hear you, loud and clear.*
AMEN.

You will turn back to me and ask for help, and I will answer your prayers.

Jeremiah 29:12 CEV

UP, UP, AND AWAY!

He gives a helping hand to everyone who falls.
The Lord loves good people.
PSALM 146:8 CEV

In 1783 the Montgolfier brothers launched the first hot air balloon to carry humans. In the years since

then, the mechanics of the process remain the same. Fill the balloon with hot air, sustain pressure with an energy source, and keep the weight within limits.

Living in God's presence is like flying a hot air balloon. When you fill your life with the breath of God, keep his words flowing in, and let go of the cares of this world, you can freely enter into the best of God's plans for your life. Living in God's presence allows you to experience a freedom unhindered by the cares of this world.

Heavenly God, as I seek your presence in my life,
give me a glimpse of your plans for me.
Allow me to see what you see.
AMEN.

Everyone will see the wonderful splendor of the L ORD *our God.*

Isaiah 35:2 CEV

IN THE RIGHT PLACE

The good news tells how God accepts everyone who has
faith, but only those who have faith.
ROMANS 1:17 CEV

The hiker had been lost on the mountain for several days. She'd kept her wits about her, however, staying dry beneath an overhang, collecting rainwater  to drink, and rationing a chocolate bar in her pack. She'd done what she knew to do and was found safe and sound.

Just like the hiker, you need to do what you know to do when things go wrong. The Bible gives specific instructions from God, including keeping your faith strong. When you allow doubt to invade your faith life, you are inviting calamity. Seek shelter under God's protection, allow your spirit to be washed with God's love for you, and partake daily of his word, your daily bread.

God has said he will never leave you or forsake you.
If you are feeling lost, consider what you need
to do to move back into his presence.

My soul, wait in silence for God only,
for my hope is from Him.

Psalm 62:5 NASB

BRAGGING RIGHTS

Some boast in chariots and some in horses, but we will boast in the name of the Lord, our God.
PSALM 20:7 NASB

In Bible times, the Israelites faced many enemies who were better equipped and better trained than

they were. Several times, God purposely had them fight an opponent who far outnumbered them. His purpose was to remind his children that they did not win the battle; he had won it for them.

When the odds are not in your favor, and it looks like there is no way you can win the battle, consider the children of Israel. Outnumbered, with primitive weapons, they called on God to save them. Boast in God, not in your own abilities, and watch God win your battles for you.

When things look bad, bring the sacrifice of praise to God and let him work through you to victory.

God, your God, is right there with you, fighting with you against your enemies, fighting to win.

Deuteronomy 20:4 MSG

IN THE QUIET

Be still, and know that I am God.
PSALM 46:10 NKJV

When you go fishing, one of the important things to remember is to be quiet. Because fish can hear you walking and talking, they generally won't bite if they suspect there is a human being attached to even the

tastiest bait you offer. Being quiet lets you catch more fish.

Being quiet before God requires you to get away from the distractions of life and allow him to speak to your soul. Work, family, television, even the cares of the day can intrude on that reflective time and interfere with how well you can hear what God is saying. Stop, listen, and reflect on what God says to you. Many times, you hear God the loudest in the quiet.

Precious God, thank you for inviting me to spend time with you. I treasure our moments together, and I commit to setting aside time to listen to you.
AMEN.

The Lord your God is in your midst, a mighty one who will save; he will rejoice over you with gladness; he will quiet you by his love.

Zephaniah 3:17 ESV

GOD WITH US

*Look, the home of God is now among his people! He
will live with them, and they will be his people.*
REVELATION 21:3 NLT

In some cultures, it is common for several generations of the same family to live in the same house.
Growing up in this setting bonds a family together, as

they live as one unit. The
older teach the younger,
and the younger are able
to care for the older.

God has also chosen
to live among his family.
As a member of that
extended household, oth-
ers strengthen and support you. You are able to teach
and be taught, comfort and be comforted, nurture
and be nurtured. God designed families as a symbol
of his desire to be in unity with you. Take joy in
belonging to the family of God.

*Loving God, thank you that I am a part of your family.
I am blessed daily by the other members,
and, in turn, we seek to bless you.*
AMEN.

Jesus, who makes people holy, and all those who are made holy have the same Father. That is why Jesus isn't ashamed to call them brothers and sisters.

Hebrews 2:11 GOD'S WORD

LIVING IN GOD'S SAFETY

We will rejoice in your salvation, and in
the name of our God we will set up
our banners! May the Lord
fulfill all your petitions.

Psalm 20:5 NKJV

FOREVER AND EVER

They entered into the covenant to seek the Lord God
of their fathers with all their heart and soul.
2 CHRONICLES 15:12 NASB

Covenant is an old-fashioned word implying formality, commitment, and longevity. Entering into covenant brings security, as each party knows that the other party has his best interests at heart. But it also brings responsibility; each party commits to fulfilling his part of the covenant.

Just as being in covenant benefits both parties to the agreement, being in covenant with God brings many benefits. The Bible says that health, prosperity, and long life are part of God's promises for you. Rest in the sure knowledge that God's best is best for you. Commit to this relationship by spending time with him, getting to know him better.

God, remind me that with you is the safest place to be.
Put me back on the path when I falter, and
hide me beneath your wings.
AMEN.

*I will establish My covenant between Me
and you and your descendants after you
in their generations, for an everlasting
covenant, to be God to you and your
descendants after you.*

Genesis 17:7 NKJV

HOLY LIVES

Be holy because I am holy.
LEVITICUS 11:44 GOD'S WORD

When you consider all of the things you have learned to do in your life, you will probably realize that most of your learning came through imitation.

You watched someone else ride a bicycle and then you tried it for yourself. You learned to dance by watching someone who knew how to dance.

To learn to live a holy life, you will need to watch the only Holy One, God. He sets before you an example of holy living in his son, Jesus. Jesus did and said what his father did and said, and he was in perfect peace at all times. Follow his example, choosing to live a life that imitates God.

It is easy to duplicate almost anything when you have the blueprints. Choose God's blueprints for your life, and watch him build you into his image.

Beloved, do not imitate what is evil, but what is good. The one who does good is of God.

3 John 1:11 NASB

NEVER FEAR

*Don't be afraid! Stand still and you
will see the LORD save you today.*
EXODUS 14:13 NLT

When hiking in bear country, there are several important instructions to follow. Don't wear anything

scented. Make lots of noise as you go through brush. The most important advice is to not run if you see a bear. Stand still. Then back slowly away, even though your initial reaction is to run from danger or threat.

When you stand still, you can assess the situation. Facing a threat face on will strengthen your resolve. God created you to be victorious in all situations. So the next time you feel under attack, stand in God's promises to you. Breathe in his presence.

*Attackers expect you to run from them. Facing them
confuses them and will give you the element of surprise.*

*I am with you, and no one is
going to attack and harm you,
because I have many people.*

Acts 18:10 NIV

SPRINGS OF ABUNDANCE

*O God, you are my God, earnestly I seek you; my soul
thirsts for you, my body longs for you, in a dry and
weary land where there is no water.*

PSALM 63:1 NIV

During the rainy season, a cactus stores water
inside its limbs to use in times of drought. Many birds
and animals are drawn to the safety of a cactus, and

there are several types of birds that
nest directly in the cactus and drink
the water stored inside.

Jesus described himself as the
Living Water. He said that if you
drink from him, you would never
thirst again. Coming to the well
during the desert times in your life
will refresh you and give you the strength to refresh
others. Water yourself daily by spending time in
God's presence, and find those springs of abundance
overflowing into all areas of your life. And let that
abundance flow over into the lives of others.

*God, show me your springs of abundance.
Flood me in your goodness and mercy.*
AMEN.

*He turned the desert into pools
of water and the parched
ground into flowing springs.*

Psalm 107:35 NIV

AN IMPORTANT PIECE
OF THE PUZZLE

*You have shown me the path to life, and you
make me glad by being near me. Sitting at
your right side, I will always be joyful.*
PSALM 16:11 CEV

In a new job, there are many things to learn. You
learn the company's policies and procedures, the specific tasks of your position, and you also begin to

understand some of the relationships and politics of the
company. Fitting into the corporate culture can be as important as doing your job well.

Living in God's presence
requires learning about God,
his will for your life, and your part in his plan.
Learning to live and work with God's family is
important, as is learning how to recruit new people
into the family. God has designed his family with you
in mind—you are an integral part of his plan.

*Holy God, thank you for including me in your
wonderful kingdom. I want to be in your
presence always—show me how to do that.*
AMEN.

The righteous will shine like the sun in the kingdom of their Father.

Matthew 13:43 NIV

NO FEAR

I'm proud to praise God; fearless now,
I trust in God. What can mere mortals do?
PSALM 56:4 MSG

When David stood before Goliath, no one believed he could win. He was a young boy, not a sol-

dier. Goliath towered over him, and all David carried were some rocks and a slingshot. Still, David remembered his past victories—when the lion and the bear had attacked his flock, he had killed them. These victories strengthened his resolve, knowing that God was on his side.

Your past will dictate your future. Remember your successes, especially the times when it was obvious that God was working in you and through you, and you will be more likely to succeed. Nothing is bigger than God, and with him, you are invincible.

Past victories in God remind you of his love for you.
God doesn't win unless you win.

You and your followers will always be successful, because God fights on your side.

1 Chronicles 12:18 CEV

GOD OF WONDERS

Take a good look at God's wonders—
they'll take your breath away.
PSALM 66:5 MSG

The fireworks explode overhead, lighting up the night sky. You ooh and aah as each subsequent display seems more elaborate than the one before. The tempo increases as the show reaches its climax, culminating in a magnificent display that can be seen for miles.

While fireworks are a sight to see, how much more so are the wonders God has created for you to enjoy? The sunrise, moonlight, even the gentle flutter of a butterfly's wings were all created by the hand of a loving God. He gives these wonders to remind you of his presence and his power. All one needs to do is step back and look around to enjoy some of God's wonders.

Loving God, thank you for thinking of me when you
created this world, and for sending reminders
to me each day of your love and care for me.
AMEN.

We are God's masterpiece. He has created us anew in Christ Jesus, so that we can do the good things he planned for us long ago.

Ephesians 2:10 NLT

SPECIALLY CHOSEN

*God has anointed you, pouring out the oil of
joy on you more than on anyone else.*
HEBREWS 1:9 NLT

Anointing oil is mentioned several times in
Scripture to describe how much God cares about you.
This special liquid was used by shepherds to heal their

sheep, to protect them from
insects, and to make their wool
more valuable.

You are God's special prize,
chosen by him. God pours his
Holy Spirit on you the way a shepherd anoints his sheep, healing
you from problems of this world,
protecting you from attacks of the
enemy, and making you an important part of his plan
to share him with the world. You are valuable to God,
and so he invests himself in you. Take joy in the
anointing and seek it every day.

*A shepherd liberally pours anointing oil on his sheep
because he knows that they will rub up against other
sheep and that some of the anointing will transfer. Share
the blessing of God's anointing with someone else today.*

*We will give you a share of the good
things the Lord gives us.*

Numbers 10:32 <small>CEV</small>

SONGS OF PRAISE

Several years ago, a large fast-food franchise admitted that it purposely vented the smell of food

cooking from its kitchens at particular times during the day to encourage passersby to come in to eat. The smell made people feel hungry for a hamburger. The concept worked. Sales increased, and other franchises quickly adopted this policy.

Sharing God with others comes from getting the message out to them that you have something they want. Peace in the midst of chaos, cheerfulness when faced with adversity, gentleness in a busy task—all are characteristics of God that are better experienced than just talked about.

Live out your relationship with God. In everything you do, remember other people are watching you. Make your life a positive statement about God.

We pray this in order that you may live a life
worthy of the Lord and may please him in
every way: bearing fruit in every good work,
growing in the knowledge of God.

Colossians 1:10 NIV

GROWING IN GRANDEUR

I am like a green olive tree in the house of God;
I trust in the mercy of God forever and ever.
PSALM 52:8 NKJV

There aren't many green plants in a desert. For most of the year, rainfall is nonexistent, and the plant growth turns brown from the blowing dust and lack of moisture. In the spring, however, all that changes, as the rain falls and life comes back into the dormant plants. Leaves sprout, flowers bloom, and fruit appears.

Living in God's presence is like living in perpetual spring. Every day is new and bright, with the gentle rains of God washing over you. Life blossoms within you, and you begin to grow spiritually, bursting forth into what God created you to be. Rejoice in his presence, and praise him for his blessings.

God, I thank you for your blessings that wash over me like
a gentle spring rain, cleansing me, refreshing me,
renewing me into your likeness and image.
AMEN.

Restore us to You, O Lord, that we may be restored; renew our days as of old.

Lamentations 5:21 NASB

UNDER CONSTRUCTION

God's plan for the world stands up,
all his designs are made to last.
PSALM 33:11 MSG

The Empire State Building was built in 1930 at the height of the Great Depression. Although impres-sive in its construction, a shortage of funds resulted in a building only half the size of the original plan. An architect designed the building, including every detail from the foundation to the dome cap, and everything in between. This building was built to last.

God has plans for your life to last eternally and to make a difference. He thought of you before the beginning of time and has continued to think of you every moment since. His plan never overlooks even the smallest detail, and everything he does has an eternal purpose.

Rest in God's plan, trust that he has everything under control, and know that you are still a work in process.

*Every house is built by someone, but
God is the builder of everything.*

Hebrews 3:4 NIV

OBEDIENCE CLASS

We are righteous when we obey all the commands
the LORD our God has given us.
DEUTERONOMY 6:25 NLT

Equine dressage competitions pit horse-and-rider teams in various maneuvers, which take discipline, commitment, and many hours of repetition to learn.

There is a right way to do each separate element, and the judges are diligent to ensure that only the best work is recognized.

Obedience to God requires discipline, commitment, and often, many tries to get it right. Thankfully, however, you do not serve a God who watches for you to make a mistake. You serve a loving God who works with you to make sure you succeed. God knows that living in his presence is your goal, not just for the moment, but for a lifetime.

Loving God, thank you for being with me as I walk this
road of faith. Make your will clear to me, so that I can be
all you want me to be.
AMEN.

*If righteous people listen and serve him,
they will live out their days in prosperity
and their years in comfort.*

Job 36:11 GOD'S WORD

SPECIAL GIFT

God planned to give us something very special
so that we would gain eternal life.
HEBREWS 11:40 GOD'S WORD

The first Fabergé egg was made as a gift for Maria, the Czarina of Russia, from Alexander III, her husband. Each egg contained a surprise, ranging

 from miniature portraits to finely jeweled replicas of palaces, carriages, and statues. Fifty-six imperial eggs were created, although twelve of them have been lost through the years.

What a blessing to know that God's gift of eternal life, as demonstrated by his love for you through Jesus, cannot be lost, misplaced, or stolen. His gift cannot be replicated with inferior materials, nor can they be forged to deceive. God's gift is everlasting, is promised by him, and is fulfilled by him.

Let God surprise you daily with his abundant love and
blessings for you. Make him the center of your life.

Do what God's teaching says; when you only listen and do nothing, you are fooling yourselves.

James 1:22 NCV

FILING A FLIGHT PLAN

Commit to the LORD whatever you do,
and your plans will succeed.
PROVERBS 16:3 NIV

Pilots file a flight plan before flying, recording where they are going, when they expect to get there, the route they will take, and what radio frequency

they will use. This information lets each control tower know what to expect, and it helps the pilot stay on course, so they get where they're going.

God is the pilot of your life. He has already shown you his flight plan—the Bible. Through it you know your ultimate destination. The Bible also helps you stay on track as you compare your walk of faith with God's directions. Following his flight plan provides you with the greatest safety and will always ensure success.

God, show me how to live my life according
to your plan for me. Show me how to
incorporate your will into my every day.
AMEN.

We will give you a share of the good things the Lord gives us.

Numbers 10:32 CEV

LIVING IN
GOD'S FAMILY

Be imitators of God, therefore,
as dearly loved children.

Ephesians 5:1 NIV

COMPLETE TRUST

Hezekiah trusted in the LORD, the God of Israel. There
was never another king like him in the land of
Judah, either before or after his time.
2 KINGS 18:5 NLT

Being called careless conjures up images of being
inadequate to the task at hand. Careless usually
means the person doesn't care about the outcome. In

Hezekiah's case, however, the
original Hebrew word for *trust*
meant "careless." He had no
cares; he trusted implicitly in
God's leading in his life. And
Hezekiah was commended for
that.

When you become care-
less, when you are able to give all your worries and
concerns to God, he will care for you. His character
shows that, and the Bible promises that. When you
trust God completely, you hand over control of your
life to one who is much better equipped to make the
right choices.

Just as a shepherd leads his sheep to good pasture, God
leads you to a life complete in him. Listen to God's
leading in your life, and let him be your guide.

Live carefree before God; he
is most careful with you.

1 Peter 5:7 MSG

SAFE IN HIM

Do not cast me away from Your presence and
do not take Your Holy Spirit from me.
PSALM 51:11 NASB

In some cultures, there are people who live in the city dump, scavenging through the trash for food to

eat and commodities they can sell to make a living. Called "dump people" by the locals, they are considered the lowest level in the social structure. For most of them, there is no way out as they live in hopelessness.

God's plan is for you to rest in him, safe, secure, protected. In God, there is always hope as you choose to live in his presence, grow into his likeness, and share him with those around you. Choose God; choose hope.

Holy God, in you I know there is safety for the present,
security for the future, and salvation from the past.
AMEN.

We have this confidence
as a sure and strong
anchor for our lives.

Hebrews 6:19 GOD'S WORD

A BRAND-NEW DIET

People need more than bread for their life;
they must feed on every word of God.
MATTHEW 4:4 NLT

Every time you turn around, it seems like you hear about a new weight-loss plan. Each diet  promises you can lose pounds and inches without any work on your part. The truth, however, is that many of these diets will not keep you healthy in the long run.

Just as eating the right combination of foods will keep you healthy, you must ingest God's food to stay spiritually healthy. Just as physical food feeds your physical body, spiritual food feeds your spiritual self. Partake of God's food—the Bible—every day. Spend time in study, in fellowship with other believers, and in prayer.

Choose a time during the day when you can spend some uninterrupted time with God, whether for five minutes or thirty. God's presence will make you hungry for more.

*You shall be called the priests of the Lord,
they shall speak of you as the ministers of
our God; you shall eat the wealth of the
nations, and in their glory you shall boast.*

Isaiah 61:6 <small>ESV</small>

STAYING ON TRACK

I walk in the way of righteousness,
in the paths of justice.
PROVERBS 8:20 ESV

A track-and-field runner is assigned a particular lane for the race. Airplanes are assigned runways by the control tower, cars drive in designated lanes, and pedestrian paths are meant for—well, pedestrians. Whenever this order isn't maintained, disorder exists and accidents can happen.

God has set a path before you, too, to maintain order and keep you safe. Living according to the Bible sets you on the right course. When you live in God's way and in his order, you not only keep yourself safe, but you also show others the right way to live.

Think of God's righteousness as the road before you, well marked with signs from the Bible and well lit with words of encouragement from those who have gone before you.

*Thanks be to God! He gives us the victory
through our Lord Jesus Christ.*

1 Corinthians 15:57 NIV

OVERFLOWING

*May the God of hope fill you with all joy and peace
in believing, so that you will abound in hope
by the power of the Holy Spirit.*
ROMANS 15:13 NASB

Spring brings warmer weather, new life, and lots
of running water. From the smallest trickle over a
 stone, to the thundering of a
magnificent waterfall, water is
abundant. Stored in the
mountains all winter as snow
and ice, the sun releases the
water to nourish the land.

If you've been going
through a cold spell in your relationship with God,
allow the Holy Spirit to break down the ice in your
heart. When you open your life to God, he will nourish you with his mercy and grace. Let the warmth of
God's love fill your life, so you may abound in hope,
joy, and peace.

*Just as the water that travels to the ocean is recycled back
into the ecosystem as life-bringing rain, your joy will
flow over into the lives of those around you.*

All kinds of fruit trees will grow on both sides of the river. . . . Each month they will produce fresh fruit because this water flows from the holy place.

Ezekiel 47:12 GOD'S WORD

NOT LETTING GO

I'm holding fast to my integrity and not loosening my grip—and, believe me, I'll never regret it.

JOB 27:6 MSG

High-wire aerialists fly through the air, catching the trapeze as it comes toward them. Timing is everything; if one of the team is out of synch, it could mean disaster for everyone. The number one rule: no matter what, don't let go of the bar.

Your integrity can be like a trapeze bar. Letting go of it, or being in the wrong place at the wrong time, invites disaster. God knows how tempting it is to give in or give up; that's why he calls you into his presence on a daily basis. When you're with him, you're always safe. Desire his presence above all else. Cling to him.

I know that in you, God, there is safety. Draw me into your presence daily, and remind me of how safe I am with you.
AMEN.

Do not be afraid of sudden fear nor of the onslaught of the wicked when it comes; for the Lord will be your confidence and will keep your foot from being caught.

Proverbs 3:25–26 NASB

PROMISES FULFILLED

The one who keeps God's word is the person in whom we see God's mature love. This is the only way to be sure we're in God.
1 John 2:5 MSG

You make many promises throughout your lifetime: you promise to be faithful to your spouse, you promise to take your kids to the zoo, you promise yourself that you will lose that extra five pounds.

God takes very seriously the promises you make to him. He gauges your spiritual maturity by how well you keep your word. The good news is that God doesn't end your relationship with him if you break a promise. He gently reminds you and then shows you a better way. What a joy to serve a loving God who wants you to mature in him.

Think about the last promise you made to someone important to you, and then determine if you have fulfilled it. If you haven't fulfilled it yet, perhaps it isn't too late now.

You belong to Christ, you are now part of Abraham's family, and you will be given what God has promised.

Galatians 3:29 CEV

SING HIS PRAISES

*I will give to the Lord the thanks due to his
righteousness, and I will sing praise to the
name of the Lord, the Most High.*

PSALM 7:17 ESV

It's easy to find people who seem worthy of your praise—sports stars, movie idols, musicians, and

superheroes. And yet, when you carefully consider their lives and the difference they have made in the lives of others, most fall drastically short of who you thought they were.

God alone is worthy of your praise. He created all you see from nothing. He set you here, now, to make a difference. God alone is interested enough in you to spend time with you continually, to answer your calls for help, and to give you what you need. Choose to praise the God of the universe. Compared to him, nothing else even comes close.

*Thank you, God, that you care enough about me to
consider me worthy to give you praise. I choose you
now, God, above all else this world can offer.*
AMEN.

*What joy for those you choose to bring near,
those who live in your holy courts. What
joys await us inside your holy Temple.*

Psalm 65:4 NLT

ABLE TO WITHSTAND
THE STORM

The LORD has planted them like strong and
graceful oaks for his own glory.
ISAIAH 61:3 NLT

God created oak trees to be able to withstand
storms. Solid trunks support supple branches that

bend with the wind; deep root sys-
tems anchor the trees solidly against
wind and water; and their seed, the
acorns, are protected inside hard
shells that can withstand drought,
fire, and trampling.

God created you, too, to be able
to withstand the storms that come
into your life. He created you in his image to withstand the events of the day that pummel you, the
chaos and confusion all around you. In him, you are
able to survive. And in surviving, you glorify him.

There is no victory without a battle. When you are
in the middle of a struggle, remember that
your victory will bring glory to God.

You give us victory over our enemies,
you put our adversaries to shame.

Psalm 44:7 NIV

ON BEING A GOOD EXAMPLE

Lead me, O LORD, in your righteousness because of my enemies—make straight your way before me.
PSALM 5:8 NIV

On "Bring a Friend to Church Day," the Sunday school teacher noticed that the regular attendees were

much better behaved than usual. When she asked one child, he said that he wanted to set the example for his friend whom he had brought with him.

Setting an example for those around you is important, but more important is knowing that God is always there with you. His presence in your life shapes your actions and your words and causes you to want to be a role model for others. As you seek God on a daily basis, remind yourself of your goal: a deeper relationship with God.

God, remind me that you don't hide how much you love me, and show me how to extend that in your name to everyone I meet.
AMEN.

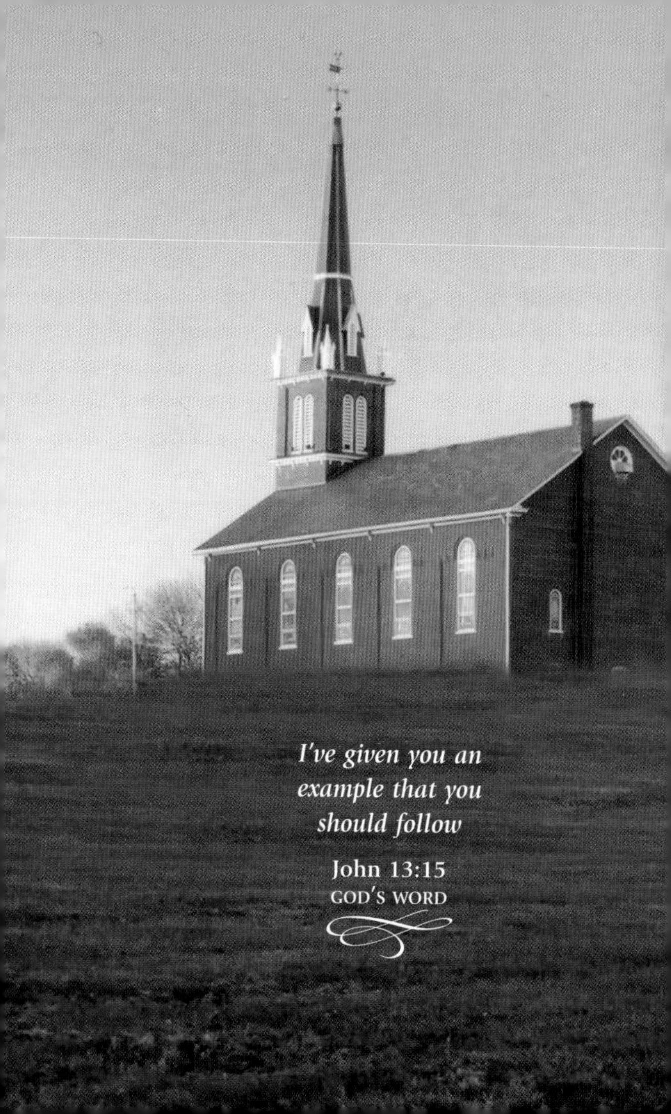

*I've given you an
example that you
should follow*

John 13:15
GOD'S WORD

I AM YOURS

I offer you my heart, Lord God, and I trust you.
PSALM 25:1–2 CEV

The patient was wheeled into the operating room to undergo surgery. As the anesthesia was being administered, the surgeon came into the room. The

patient whispered, "I hope you're in good form today, Doc. My life is in your hands."

It isn't easy to give control of your life over to someone else. God knows that. He knows the struggle you go through each and every day to trust in him completely. That's why he sent the Holy Spirit as friend and counselor. That's why he gives you friends and family. Trust God to know what is best for you, every moment.

Just as surgery can be a matter of life and death, so is your decision to allow God to take control of your life. You can allow him free rein; he loves you too much to mess up.

*Jesus said to his disciples, "Don't be worried!
Have faith in God and have faith in me."*

John 14:1 CEV

GOD IS FAITHFUL

*You, Lord, are my God! I will praise you for doing
the wonderful things you had planned and
promised since ancient times.*

ISAIAH 25:1 CEV

The quarterback threw the ball, his teammates
scattering in all directions according to the play he
had just called. Unfortunately, the other team was

prepared and intercepted the ball.
While the plan was good and the play
was perfectly executed, it still failed.

No matter how well thought-out
your plans are, they, too, will fail.
Without God, nothing lasts forever.
Only in him and through him will
you be able to achieve anything that
will last beyond this life. God has promised that he is
faithful. He has proven himself and continues to
prove himself. God is dependable.

*Everlasting God, you have shown yourself to be the only
one I can truly count on. Make me as faithful as you are.*
AMEN.

The LORD is faithful. The Holy One of Israel has chosen you.

Isaiah 49:7 GOD'S WORD

SOARING LIKE AN EAGLE

For you who fear my name, the Sun of Righteousness
will rise with healing in his wings.
MALACHI 4:2 NLT

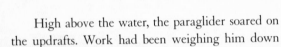

High above the water, the paraglider soared on the updrafts. Work had been weighing him down lately, and everything had seemed to bother him. But up there, he could leave his cares behind and concentrate on flying. With each subsequent updraft lifting his glider, his spirits were also lifted. He felt truly free for the first time in months.

You, too, can leave your cares and worries behind. In God, you can soar like an eagle, lifted high to his presence. God calls you to himself, desiring to fill you with his essence, to calm your fears, and to heal you. You can experience true freedom with God.

Paragliders soar because they have more lift than
load. Give your load to God, and let him
lift you high into his presence.

You will find happiness by worshiping him.

Job 22:26 CEV

PERFECT FREEDOM

*You have been set free from sin and have
become slaves to righteousness.*
ROMANS 6:18 NIV

Not many years ago, zoos were like a cage-lined
path, where the specimens were restricted to areas

about the size of a small bed-
room. Today's zoos place the
animals in a setting similar to
their original habitat in the wild.
However, while the animals
may look like they are free, they
are still captives.

Living in God is the only
true freedom there is. Choosing to live in this freedom
means that barriers that keep others captive are
removed, allowing you to become the person God
planned for you to be. As you live free in God, he lives
freely in you.

*You must choose whom you want to be free in.
Choosing God is choosing life.*

*Choose for yourselves this day
whom you will serve.*

Joshua 24:15 NIV

Living in
Relationship
with God

Everyone who wins the victory will inherit these things. I will be their God, and they will be my children.

Revelation 21:7 GOD'S WORD

WHEN YOUR EYES ARE OPENED

*The LORD looks down from heaven on the
sons of men to see if there are any who
understand, any who seek God.*

PSALM 14:2 NIV

Kittens are born with their eyes closed. Because
they cannot see, they stick close to their mother. They

bond with her, learning from
her. Their eyes open when
they are physically able to
begin the maturing process.

Being born into God's
family is similar. At first, you
don't understand your part in
the family. All you know is the presence of God, and
you learn to recognize his voice. As you mature, God
reveals himself and your part in the family to you a little at a time, as you are ready. When you understand
God's purpose for your life—when your eyes are
opened—you are able to participate in his plan.

*Father God, I praise you for including me in your family.
As I seek you, you reveal yourself to me. Create in
me a hunger and thirst for more of you.*
AMEN.

Because I have done what is right, I will see you. When I awake, I will be fully satisfied, for I will see you face to face.

Psalm 17:15 NLT

WATER IN THE DESERT PLACES

*Set yourselves apart for a holy life. Live a holy life,
because I am God, your God.*
LEVITICUS 20:7 MSG

When you think of the desert and valuable commodities, you probably think of oil. In fact, water is
the most valuable resource in a desert. In Bible times,

wells were carefully protected so
that when the owner returned
that way, the water would be
available.

You are a most valuable com-
modity to God. He carefully protects you from those who would
steal your joy, your health, and
your faith. Spending time with him is one way to
make sure that you are secure in him. God has invest-
ed a lot of time in you and is determined not to lose
you.

*Just as water is carried in containers, God encloses
his Holy Spirit in you; you carry his presence
to the far ends of the earth.*

I will make springs in the desert, so that
my chosen people can be refreshed.

Isaiah 43:20 <small>NLT</small>

MERCIFUL LOVE

The LORD loves righteousness and justice.
His mercy fills the earth.
PSALM 33:5 GOD'S WORD

The condemned prisoner stood before the judge and jury, his eyes downcast. He had done what they accused him of, and he had been convicted of his

crime. Now he was throwing himself on the mercy of the court, asking them to not sentence him to death, even though he knew he deserved to die.

When you first chose to include God in your life, you came to him as a condemned prisoner. You asked for, and received, his mercy when you didn't really deserve it. As you continue your walk of faith, there will be situations where you will doubt your right to ask for more mercy. Never doubt God's love for you—his love is so full that it fills the whole earth.

Forgiving God, when I forget, remind me of your
bountiful love for me, and show me ways
to share that love with others.
AMEN.

The Lord's lovingkindnesses indeed never cease, for His compassions never fail. They are new every morning; great is Your faithfulness.

Lamentations 3:22–23 NASB

BLESSINGS

He who pursues righteousness and love
finds life, prosperity and honor.
PROVERBS 21:21 NIV

It's always exciting to receive a gift. Whether it's a special occasion, such as your birthday, or something completely unexpected, gifts show you that someone thought you were special and that you were being thought about.

God's presence in your life is a gift from God, reminding you that he thinks about you all the time. God's presence brings with it all of the characteristics of God, including more abundant life, prosperity in all its forms, and honor. God thinks you are so special that he desires to be with you always. Show him how special you think he is by wanting to always be in his presence.

God of all that is good, I want all of you. Show me
how to seek you in every way, to experience
you every day, and to grow closer to you.
AMEN.

It is my pleasure to tell you about the miraculous signs and wonders that the Most High God has performed for me.

Daniel 4:2 NIV

KEEP THE HOME FIRES BURNING

*I have kept the ways of the Lord; I have not
done evil by turning from my God.*
2 Samuel 22:22 NIV

There is a song that was written during World
War I as an encouragement to soldiers and their families. The song reminds the listener of the sacrifices

being made, both in lives
and in time apart. It also
encourages soldiers' wives to
continue to believe that their
husbands were coming home,
no matter how bad it looked.

Sometimes it can be
difficult to live a holy and
faith-filled life. When you
feel discouraged, remember that God knows what
you're going through and is right there with you.
Continue steadfast in what you know is the right
thing to do, and see God at work in your life, fulfilling his promises to you.

*Very few battles will last for years; most last only days or
hours. Remain strong in your faith, and see God at work
in you, in your life, and in the lives of those around you.*

I am the Lord God of Judah, and I will have mercy and save Judah by my own power—not by wars and arrows or swords and cavalry.

Hosea 1:7 CEV

REWARD OFFERED FOR
SAFE RETURN

*Our Lord, keep showing love to everyone who
knows you, and use your power to save
all whose thoughts please you.*

PSALM 36:10 CEV

All over the neighborhood, signs were posted about the lost dog. "Reward Offered" was in large letters, followed by a phone number and the statement "we miss our dog." They didn't care if the dog ran away or wandered too far. They just wanted their dog back.

In the same way, God has put up signs for you. He has given you a second chance to come back home to him. So whether you ran from him, or just wandered off a little at a time, know that God wants you back. Spend time with him today, and allow him to tell you just how important you are to him.

*When you truly treasure a thing, you want it with you
all the time. That's how God feels about you—
show him how much you treasure him by
being with him all the time.*

*You are precious in my eyes,
and honored, and I love you.*

Isaiah 43:4 ESV

HARD HAT AREA

*Each morning he'll pull on sturdy work clothes
and boots, and build righteousness and
faithfulness in the land.*
Isaiah 11:5 MSG

Steel-toed boots, safety goggles, and hard hats are mandatory on construction sites. While steel-toed  boots aren't a fashion statement, the worker who drops a block of concrete on his toes is very happy that the boots do the job they were intended to do—protect him.

God is your protective clothing: he makes your paths safe so you won't stumble; he guards your eyes from things you shouldn't see; and he covers you with his salvation. God protects you as he builds you up into a sure and solid image of himself, able to take on anything that the world can throw at you.

*Loving God, thank you that you care enough for me to
protect me. Keep me safe under your shelter
and hold me gently in your loving hands.*
AMEN.

Rescue me from my enemies, O my God.
Protect me from those who attack me.

Psalm 59:1 GOD'S WORD

RULING IN HIS PLACE

God's kingdom consists of God's approval and peace, as well as the joy that the Holy Spirit gives.
ROMANS 14:17 GOD'S WORD

The ship had sunk quickly, and they'd been lucky to get off in time. Still, afloat in an open raft on the ocean wasn't the best place to be. All around them was water, but none to drink. The waters swarmed

with fish, with no way to catch them. It seemed ironic that they might die of thirst and hunger in the midst of such plenty.

Trying to find peace and joy anywhere else except in God is much the same: You will be kept busy, but you will always be hungry. Peace and joy are the characteristics of a life lived in God's presence; they are not things you acquire. Seek God, and you will automatically have the peace and joy your spirit craves.

Just as being dehydrated causes you to crave water, so does a God-deficiency cause you to crave his presence. Seek him daily, and fill yourself full with him.

You gave them bread from heaven when
they were hungry and water from the
rock when they were thirsty.
Nehemiah 9:15 NLT

A TASTE OF WHAT'S TO COME

*The Spirit of God whets our appetite by giving us a
taste of what's ahead. He puts a little of heaven in
our hearts so that we'll never settle for less.*
2 CORINTHIANS 5:5 MSG

At a recent fair, merchants offered tasty tidbits of
their wares. Not enough to satisfy your hunger; their

purpose was to create a hunger in
you so you would buy the full
meal. They knew that once you
got a little taste, you would want
more.

God allows you to see a little
of him at a time, creating a
hunger for him in your life. He
shows some of his goodness in
your life, with a promise that there is more to come.
As you spend time in his presence, you see more of his
character, which in turn makes you want more.

*All-giving God, thank you for revealing yourself
to me a little at a time. When I try to resist,
create in me a hunger for more of you.*
AMEN.

You're blessed when you've worked up a good appetite for God. He's food and drink in the best meal you'll ever eat.

Matthew 5:6 MSG

PRIESTS AND SAINTS OF GOD

Let your priests be clothed with righteousness,
and let your saints shout for joy.
PSALM 132:9 ESV

It can be pretty confusing when you watch the first rehearsals for a school play. It's difficult to distinguish between the characters, since they all seem to look alike. By the time dress rehearsal comes around,

when they are wearing their costumes, it becomes easier to tell the players apart. You recognize them from their costumes.

God's people don't wear physical clothing that separates them from others. God's people look different to others, not because of what they wear, but because of how they act. Spending time with God makes you look and act more like him. Others will recognize God in you, and they will want to know why you are different.

Doing something nice for someone reflects your
spiritual garments. Reflect on how you
want to look different to others.

In his great power God becomes like clothing to me; he binds me like the neck of my garment.

Job 30:18 NIV

SWEET DREAMS

Hope does not disappoint, because the love of God has been poured out within our hearts through the Holy Spirit who was given to us.

ROMANS 5:5 NASB

In the Old Testament a widow had less than a cup of oil, enough to make one loaf of bread.

However, when God spoke through Elijah, she made a loaf of bread for him, one for herself, and then went on to fill every jar and jug she could find with the oil provided by God.

God filled this woman's jars because she needed oil, and he will pour his blessings into your life, into those empty areas that need to be filled. Seek God today; he is in the business of making dreams come true. He already knows what you need, and he is simply waiting for you to ask.

It's easy to trust God for the ordinary. By knowing his intimate will for your life, you can begin to trust him for the extraordinary.

God can do anything, you
know—far more than you
could ever imagine or
guess or request in your
wildest dreams!

Ephesians 3:20 MSG

ASSURANCE OF ANSWERED PRAYER

This is the confidence that we have in Him, that if we ask anything according to His will, He hears us.
1 JOHN 5:14 NKJV

When Jesus healed the blind man, the man praised God for his healing. Undoubtedly this man, blind from birth, had prayed many times and asked  God for healing. His family and friends had probably prayed too. And yet God had waited to answer their prayers.

Do you have prayers that seem unanswered? Do you sometimes worry that your requests are just not getting through? When it seems like nothing is working in the Prayer Department, don't give up. Draw closer to God than ever before. Know that he hears, that he's concerned, and that the answer is already on its way. There's no such thing as unanswered prayer with God.

There are three steps in getting your prayers answered—ask, believe, and see.

Whatever things you ask
when you pray, believe
that you receive them,
and you will have them.

Mark 11:24 NKJV

CLEAR SKIES

A ruler who obeys God and does right is like the sunrise on a cloudless day, or like rain that sparkles on the grass.
2 SAMUEL 23:3–4 CEV

When sailors are out on the ocean during a storm at night, they keep their eyes trained on the horizon.

They are looking for help, they are watching for land, and they want to see the sun as soon as it begins to rise. They know that even the bleakest moments look better when there is sunlight.

When you are caught in the storms of life, when all around the waves are rolling over you, remember this: God is there with you. He never lets you get in over your head, and he is waiting patiently for you to call on him. You can call on him through prayer, through frantic whispers, through a friend.

Heavenly God, thank you that you are my anchor through the storms, my guide in the dark. Remind me of that when I try to go my own way.
AMEN.

For anyone out there who doesn't know where you're going, anyone groping in the dark, here's what: Trust in God. Lean on your God!

Isaiah 50:10 MSG

RIGHT OF OWNERSHIP

[You] belong to God; so run from all these evil things,
and follow what is right and good. Pursue a godly life,
along with faith, love, perseverance, and gentleness.
1 TIMOTHY 6:11 NLT

When you own something, you want to take good care of it. You expect it to fulfill the purpose you bought it for, whether that be safety, security, or fun. Ownership means that something belongs to you.

Belonging to God's family brings with it rights and responsibilities. You have the right to claim ownership in those things that belong to God, such as faith, love, perseverance, and gentleness. You also have a responsibility to take ownership of those things in your life. God has chosen to include you in his family because he loves you. He has designed you with a special purpose in mind that only you can fulfill.

When you demonstrate God's character in your life,
you are showing whose family you belong to.

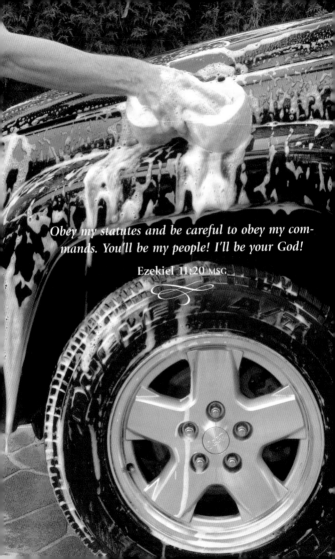

Obey my statutes and be careful to obey my commands. You'll be my people! I'll be your God!

Ezekiel 11:20 MSG

SAFETY SHIELD

My shield is God above, who saves
those whose motives are decent.
PSALM 7:10 GOD'S WORD

In the old *Star Trek* episodes, invisible power shields protected the space ships. So long as the power to generate the shields was sufficient, no weapon could penetrate. The real problem arose when the generator went off-line, causing the ship to be in jeopardy.

What a comfort to know that God's presence is the only shield you will ever need against the enemy. How powerful is your God you serve who can withstand whatever comes at you. There is no weapon big enough, no attack strong enough, no battle long enough that God will not win. And when God wins, you win. Staying in his presence ensures your victory.

God, I am so blessed that in you, I don't need to
worry about how to win this next battle. I rest
in your presence, and I call on your name,
the name that is above all names.
AMEN.

*In every battle you will need faith as
your shield to stop the fiery arrows
aimed at you by Satan.*

Ephesians 6:16 NLT

FINDING YOUR WAY

Every part of Scripture is God-breathed and useful one way or another—showing us truth, exposing our rebellion, correcting our mistakes, training us to live God's way.
2 TIMOTHY 3:16 MSG

Ants may be pests, but they are a wonderful creation of God, navigating by scent. When one ant finds a food source, it follows its trail back to the nest. Each ant then follows the trail as it goes back to the nest with the food.

The same God who devised a method for ants to find their way has made sure he left a way for you to find him. All of God's creation declares his majesty, his attention to detail, and his care for his people. When God speaks, he tells of his love for you and of his joy in what he has created for you.

Almighty God, thank you for each new morning with the promises that it brings. Remind me that this day was created by you for you.
AMEN.

This is the day which the Lord has made; let us rejoice and be glad in it.

Psalm 118:24 NASB

GETTING IT RIGHT

We don't enjoy being disciplined. It always seems to
cause more pain than joy. But later on, those who
learn from that discipline have peace that
comes from doing what is right.
HEBREWS 12:11 GOD'S WORD

When you hear that someone is being disciplined, you might conjure up an image of being punished, or you might think of that person as being strong-willed and accomplishing what they set out to do. The word *discipline* can have positive or negative connotations.

When God disciplines, he isn't punishing you for something you did wrong. Rather, he is showing you a better way to accomplish the task set before you. Learning from the correction means that the next time you won't take a wrong direction. You will get it right the first time, and, in turn, be able to show others how to get it right.

Just as a sailboat without a rudder will eventually run
aground unless there is a change of course, you will
occasionally need correction of your direction.

It's the child he loves that he disciplines;
the child he embraces, he also corrects.

Hebrews 12:6 MSG

A FATHER'S JOY

The LORD's delight is in those who honor him,
those who put their hope in his unfailing love.
PSALM 147:11 NLT

In the Bible, the Proverbs 31 woman is credited with bringing honor to her husband through her  actions. When you read about her, you find she works hard, takes care of her family, is obedient to tradition, and thinks of others before herself.

You bring honor to God in the same way. Doing your job well, caring for those who love God, being obedient to what God asks you to do, and putting others' interests before your own all show that you are different than most people. It also shows that you desire to emulate God's character, which is the best way to bring, and show, honor.

Live each day as if you were writing your own
eulogy—what would you want God and
others to say about you at your funeral?

Each generation will announce to the next
your wonderful and powerful deeds.

Psalm 145:4 CEV

In whose hand is the life of every living thing, and the breath of all mankind?

Job 12:10 NKJV

His faithful promises are your
armor and protection.

Psalm 91:4 <small>NLT</small>